T0312831

PONDS

PONDS

A practical guide to design, construction and planting

David Kerr

✳ THE CROWOOD PRESS

First published in 2023 by
The Crowood Press Ltd
Ramsbury, Marlborough
Wiltshire SN8 2HR

enquiries@crowood.com

www.crowood.com

© David Kerr, 2023

All rights reserved. No part of this publication may be reproduced or transmitted in any form or by any means, electronic or mechanical, including photocopy, recording, or any information storage and retrieval system, without permission in writing from the publishers.

British Library Cataloguing-in-Publication Data
A catalogue record for this book is available from the British Library.

ISBN 978 0 7198 4253 5

Cover design by Nikki Ellis

Typeset by Envisage IT
Printed and bound in India by Thomson Press India Ltd

CONTENTS

INTRODUCTION

ABOUT THE AUTHOR

From an early age I was growing lettuces in a mixture of heavy clay and broken concrete, but I soon became fascinated by water and all the unfamiliar and strange things that live in it. My long-suffering parents tolerated an ever-increasing number of holes appearing in their precious garden, filled with a variety of hastily constructed and poorly designed death traps in the guise of garden ponds. Slowly but surely, I began to understand why some ponds were successful and others not so much, and this learning process continues today. After achieving a degree in Zoology and a Masters in Fish Biology, I started a trout farm in Devon from scratch in 1982, while starting a popular sideline retailing aquatic plants, pond fish and pond accessories. In the winter months I constructed a wide variety of fishponds and garden ponds in connection with the expanding aquatic business. After selling the trout farm in the 1990s I moved to my current home in 2001, where I began to grow and sell aquatic plants by mail order under the name of Devon Pond Plants. This business has been tremendously successful, and I have learned a great deal more about what makes a pond work and how the different plants perform and grow. Through my website at devonpondplants.co.uk I have earned a reputation for straight talking and telling it how it is, and I will follow that strategy in this book. My aim is to cut out all the usual padding and concentrate on the main nuggets of information, adopting a practical rather than a theoretical approach. I will pass on some tips which have taken me many years to discover and share some insider knowledge which is hard to find for yourself.

ABOUT THIS BOOK

I hope that this book will allow the reader to leapfrog many of the errors commonly made and enable them

Last year The Wildlife Aid Foundation embarked on its biggest ever life-changing project, part of which was to build three massive ponds for wildlife. Seeking specialist advice on aquatic planting, we reached out to David Kerr, who, after an initial consultation, quickly set about drawing up a very comprehensive plan for the design and planting of the area. His obvious knowledge and expertise left us in no doubt that we were in good and safe hands. What a breath of fresh air!

Simon Cowell, CEO of Wildlife Aid,
and former presenter of *Wildlife SOS*.

to achieve success first time around. It is aimed at those with a reasonable level of practical ability and gardening knowledge, who nevertheless have limited experience of ponds and pond planting. It is therefore assumed that it is unnecessary to explain which tools will be necessary to dig a hole, or which way up a plant goes in the hole (green side up is a good general rule!). If you're the sort of person who needs to be told that they need a wheelbarrow and spade, and be shown a picture of these, this book may not be for you. In particular, contractors and garden designers with limited previous experience of aquatic planting may find it very useful.

The aim is to provide the detail lacking in other texts to enable the optimum planting in a pond to maximise its wildlife value and aesthetic appeal. It is not intended to cover aspects such as pumps and filters, waterfalls and fountains, hard landscaping details or fish keeping matters. A successful planting scheme depends in large part on good design, so there is a substantial section explaining the importance of careful construction before the planting is covered in detail. There is a long and detailed section on the plants which are most likely

Typha flowers.

marestail is *Hippuris*. Water willow can be *Persicaria* or *Justicia* and willow moss is *Fontinalis*. Almost everyone calls the tall marginal plants topped by brown pokers 'bulrushes', however they are in fact reed mace (*Typha*). Bulrushes (*Schoenoplectus*) have tall tubular dark green pith-filled leaves and small spikes of brown flowers. (Rushes typically have tubular type leaves, whereas reeds have flattened leaves, but people often use the terms interchangeably.) Very many local names exist for native plants, and this can add to confusion. A dictionary of Latin to common names and vice versa can be found in the Appendices at the back of the book. There you will also find various useful information tables and contacts.

to be available in the UK, together with the growing requirements of each. Practical advice relating to propagation and pond maintenance is given, and at the end there is a chapter on common problems and how to deal with them.

I make no apologies for primarily using the Latin binomial names for plants to avoid confusion; common names are given where available. The Latin binomial is given in *italics*. Common names are interesting but confusing, for example horsetail is *Equisetum* whereas

WATER IN THE LANDSCAPE

Water is not just an essential part of the landscape, or part of life. Water *is* life. Natural ponds do differ from manmade ones in many ways, but a well-constructed and planted artificial pond is a valuable addition to any garden or field. A garden or piece of land containing water is a magnet for wildlife and is infinitely richer than one without. Even within minutes of filling a new pond, insects will arrive to check it out, and that very

Water in the landscape.

Dragonfly on an iris bud.

plants that inhabit them have evolved to be able to cope with variations in water levels and indeed to be able to survive periods of total drought, while taking the opportunity during flooding to colonise new areas. Along with this strategy of colonisation and endurance comes a tendency to be fast growing, tough and invasive, so many water plants are not suitable for smaller ponds at all and need to be used with care even in very large ponds if a total takeover is to be avoided. Ponds without plants are biologically poor, even though the water quality may be excellent. In nature these are the relatively rare oligotrophic, or nutrient-poor, mountain lakes and tarns, into which little organic material finds its way. Levels of nitrates and phosphates are low, which means that plants are starved of plant food, therefore insects are mostly absent and larger animals have no food and no place to hide and reproduce. In lowland areas the input from rivers and streams carrying a high load of organic material makes ponds eutrophic, or nutrient-rich. At its extreme end this can mean that decomposition of this material produces toxic gases and other compounds which exclude the possibility of life. This is why woodland ponds are

night you can be sure that mammals will visit too. In nature, ponds are relatively short lived, geologically speaking, since they steadily fill up with sediment and plant material, morphing into bogs and heathland. They are therefore transient, and the animals and

Pond reverting to bog.

often problematic – the large quantity of fallen leaves can blanket the pond base and poison the water – but in open unwooded areas it means that there is an explosion of fast-growing plants. This in turn means that the pond rapidly silts up with organic material produced by and trapped by the plants, and in no time at all there is no pond at all, just an area of dense reed-bed and marsh.

The principal difference between a natural pond and most artificial ones is that the former is connected

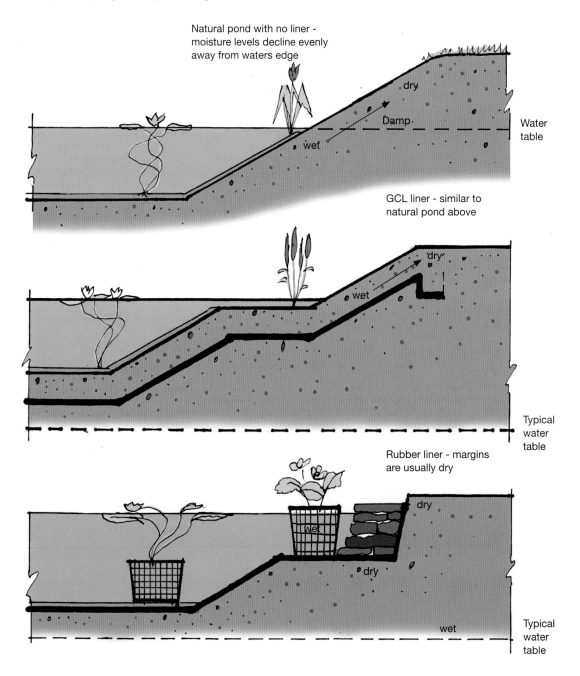

Natural pond with no liner -
moisture levels decline evenly
away from waters edge

dry

Damp·

Water table

wet

GCL liner - similar to
natural pond above

dry

wet

Typical water table

Rubber liner - margins
are usually dry

dry

wet

dry

wet

Typical water table

Progression of wetness at the margins.

hydraulically to ground water and there is a seamless progression from wet to dry at the edges, since there is no liner. This usually makes for a more variable water level, and it does not guarantee that the pond will not dry out completely when the ground water level drops. However, even if a geotextile liner is used, as typically on ponds over 200m², the pond itself is cut off from the ground water and cannot be replenished from this source. On a hot summer's day, a shallow lined pond could drop as much as 5cm from evaporation and transpiration, but ground water levels are unlikely to drop that fast, so in this way a lined pond is less stable than a natural one. In the case of on-stream ponds of course the water level will be more or less constant unless the stream dries up completely.

In hot Middle Eastern countries, the value of water is perhaps understandably appreciated more highly, and cool oases with fountains and moving water have been a feature of wealthy homes for many hundreds of years, but in Great Britain, the interest in incorporating large-scale artificial water features into private estates and gardens really only began fairly recently, with landscape architects such as Lancelot 'Capability' Brown, Gertrude Jekyll, Beth Chatto and the like. Few aquatic plants have a long history of cultivation and those that do are mostly those with practical uses such as thatching reed (*Phragmites communis*) or lotus, every part of which can be eaten in tropical or subtropical countries. The relatively low effort spent on developing new varieties of pond plants, coupled with the short history of water gardening, means that the range of commercially available aquatic plants is quite small when compared with the panoply of ordinary garden plants, and when this is combined with the need to avoid many undesirable species, it doesn't leave a vast number of possibilities for planting. A few species, such as *Caltha palustris* (kingcup or marsh marigold), could be considered to be almost essential, but for most smaller ponds on a garden scale, the range of suitable plants is quite small. It is therefore vital to select the right ones and give these plants the best possible conditions to enable them to thrive.

Perfection of landscaping.

CHAPTER 1

PRELIMINARY PLANNING

TYPES OF POND

Ponds can be artificially separated into many categories, such as 'formal pond', 'fish pond', 'swimming pond', 'wildlife pond', 'ornamental pond', 'duck pond' and so on, but any body of water will help wildlife to some extent.

Nine out of ten people, if asked, would say that the primary purpose of their pond is to encourage wildlife, but of course most also prefer to have a degree of control over the look of the pond too, and would

Formal symmetrical design.

Natural swimming pond.

A wildlife pond.

An ornamental pond.

Small wildlife pond.

Attractive wildlife pond.

want to consider it an attractive feature in the garden. Frankly, a newt doesn't care about the colour scheme and would actively prefer a dense jungle of vegetation to a manicured look, so some degree of compromise is almost always necessary. Some choose to have more than one pond, with a tidier and more visually attractive look (to them) in the foreground and a slightly more unkempt version further down the garden 'for wildlife'. Try to look at it from the point of view of the wildlife that you hope to attract. Animals require three main things: a hospitable environment in which to live, a hiding place to avoid being eaten by other animals, and something to eat themselves. It's as simple as that. There's absolutely no reason why that pond can't look attractive to human eyes too, and there is no reason for a wildlife pond to have to look scruffy.

Having said that, the most diverse habitat is created by maximising the number of niches in which animals and plants can live, so an operating theatre mentality is to be avoided in favour of a managed degree of 'LIA' – Leave It Alone. An occasional clear-up will be necessary to remove excess organic material from the pond, but a tangle of old stems is a valuable place for many insects and amphibians to lay their eggs, so don't be too quick to tidy up those fallen stems until after all the critters have completed their breeding cycle.

If you wish to maximise the appeal of the pond for wildlife, there are three important things to remember before you start:

1. Access

Animals need a safe route to get in and out of the water, so the pond should be linked by a wildlife-friendly corridor to the rest of the surroundings. The best way to ensure that is to link the pond vegetation with planted areas outside the pond, linking further to the wilder areas of the garden. A pond which is completely surrounded by paving or other hard landscaping for design purposes is less likely to attract shy wildlife. A carefully thought-out edge detail will allow easy ingress and egress (more on this later).

2. Fish

Fish do not exist in tiny natural bodies of water (which are rare in themselves) because the habitat is too small to support them. Therefore, fish are not appropriate in small wildlife ponds. Once a pond gets over about 100m^2, it can support a small number of tiny

Formal white pond.

fish such as sticklebacks or minnows, which are not at the top of the food chain themselves but actually prey items for some of the bigger insects, like dragonfly larvae and diving beetles. If you can't live without a couple of goldfish then by all means introduce them; just remember that they will eat a high proportion of all the damselfly eggs and tadpoles and you will therefore see far fewer froglets and beautiful insects. It's your pond, and at the end of the day, your choice.

3. Sun

Insects are cold-blooded and to some degree require the heat of the sun to enable them to get airborne. Flowers that have evolved to attract insects to pollinate them mostly grow best in the sun. Therefore, a successful wildlife pond will be best situated in a mostly sunny location. (*See* 'The Paradox of Shade' below.) Nearly all of the action takes place in the warmest and

Wildlife corridor.

Open, sunny location.

shallowest areas and excessive depth is unnecessary – even in the worst UK winter it is unlikely that there will be more than 15cm of ice, so a depth of 60cm is more than adequate to protect wildlife from freezing.

PLANNING AND POSITIONING

It's really important to make a plan, and the bigger the pond is, the more detailed the plan will need to be. In

Drawing a plan

At the very least it is worth preparing a scaled plan and section of the area, not forgetting to include the area immediately around the pond and how it will integrate with the rest of the garden. Do keep one copy without scribbles and annotations so you can use it as a master, producing as many copies for changes as are necessary. Use marker spray to mark the outline and check that it looks right before ever putting a spade in the ground. It's much easier to kick over an old marked line and redraw it than replace soil already dug out – it never goes back as firmly as before.

Poor design has led to too much liner showing.

the case of larger ponds requiring machine digging, a proper land survey is to be recommended.

While you're at the planning stage, bear in mind that most pond liners come in widths in multiples of 0.6m,

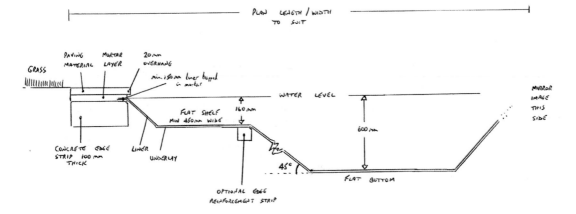

Basic sketch plan.

so sometimes it's worth considering planning the exact pond dimensions around the liner width possibilities, rather than the other way round. Sometimes people wildly overestimate the size of liner required, ending up with a huge and probably useless offcut that looks like a map of Norway. You do need to allow at least 15cm overlap all around, but you don't need to waste a metre all round.

For ponds less than one or two cubic metres a simple sketch is probably all that is necessary but do think carefully about what you will do with the excavated material. Please don't dump all the subsoil right next to the pond, stick a couple of modest sized stones in it and call it a rockery. Nothing will grow well in it, and it will look like exactly what it is. If you don't need the material to fill holes elsewhere then it

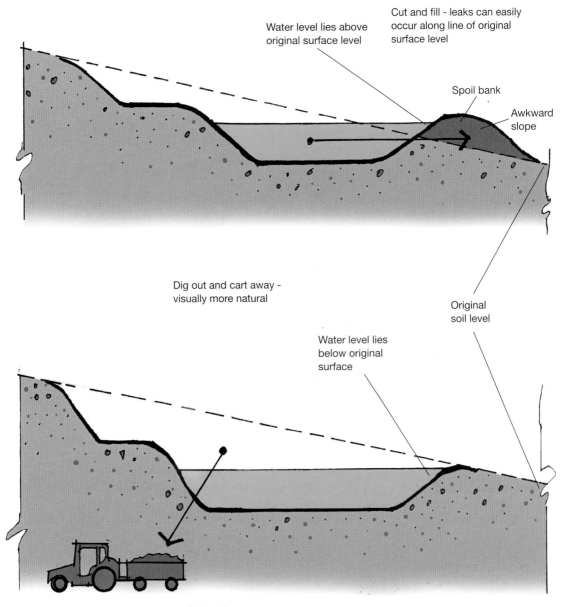

Avoid cut and fill in favour of excavate and remove.

is preferable to get a skip and have it removed. It may be annoying that this will be one of the biggest costs, but it will be the best thing you could do. With medium to large garden ponds the cost of spoil removal can start to get worrying, so by all means consider if you are able to 'lose' some of the spoil somewhere else on the site. The best way to do this is to identify an area that could be raised without causing problems, strip back the topsoil, tip and spread the unwanted subsoil and then spread the original topsoil back on top.

Making the pond look natural

The most natural looking ponds are created by excavating out of the existing landscape, removing all the spoil, not cutting and filling, which is the easiest and cheapest solution (*see* also Chapter 4). On more steeply sloping sites one needs to consider the topography very carefully. One thing to try to avoid is to create a berm or bank on the downhill side of the pond. This will make the pond look unnatural and out of place, like a reservoir. Natural ponds don't form on the side of a hill with a retaining bank on the downhill side, and it *will* show. You will also probably end up with an awkward bank and probably a steep slope to manage, and settlement or erosion issues can result. Additionally, if the topsoil is not stripped off the site where the bank resides before the material is tipped there, it creates a layer which is very vulnerable to leaking. If a liner is used, then this is not an issue.

One issue affecting most ponds is that of windblown leaves and waterborne soil and debris. It's really important to minimise the amount of organic material and soil finding its way into your pond, as this is what causes algal blooms and problems with blanket weed and duckweed. If possible, ensure that the pond is on the south to southeast side of any tall walls, fences or trees to maximise the amount of sunlight available. Don't locate the pond under or just downwind of large trees

The paradox of shade

While surface cover in a pond is vital to prevent sunlight from causing excessive algal growth, this shade should be provided by the pond plants themselves, *not* by trees or shrubs outside of the pond. Most pond plants, especially those with coloured flowers, require plenty of sun in order to flower well. The coloured flowers evolved to attract insects, and most insects need warmth and sun to be able to fly, as they are cold-blooded. Shady ponds full of leaves are very poor for wildlife and offer few planting options.

or shrubs, and don't necessarily locate it in the lowest lying part of the garden, to prevent heavy rain from washing soil from the paths and borders into the pond. Ideally, the pond should be in the sun for most of the day and should be somewhere where it can be enjoyed.

The orientation of the pond is of little consequence and is best planned to suit the space in which it sits. Do, however, give full consideration from the point of view of the wildlife that you hope will make use of the pond.

GROUND CONDITIONS

If your pond is in a low-lying part of the garden, or if there is a high water table in winter, remember Archimedes – water pressure from underneath the pond can cause 'hippos' in the liner; these can be difficult to deal with and can cause disruption to planted baskets on top. This can cause big problems with geotextile liners, which are extremely heavy and rely on tight joints filled with bentonite clay for their waterproofing. If these joints are opened up by pressure from below, they may not seal properly when the ground water subsides and will probably leak thereafter. This is a very difficult thing to fix, so consider a necklace of land drains under the liner to prevent it. It is even possible for preformed ponds to lift out of the soil if they are not full to the brim.

Making a small dam

If a stream runs through the area where your pond is to be made, even if the stream rises on your land, you may require water authority consent in the form of an abstraction and/or discharge licence. Damming a stream to create a pond is highly inadvisable in any case. It is highly recommended that you construct the pond to one side of the existing stream, or if not, construct a bypass channel to allow the whole spate flow of the stream to run around the outside of the pond while drawing off the bare minimum to keep the pond topped up. If you don't, you will find that the pond fills up with silt and debris extremely quickly, and the regular job of removing all this is likely to cost more than the original construction, not to mention the question of what you will do with it all. The amount of material carried by even a small watercourse during a flood is unbelievable, and it is much better for you if it roars all around your pond and becomes a nuisance to someone else

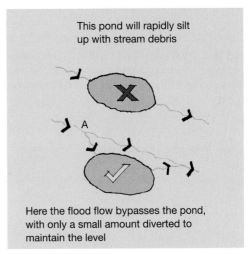

Create a bypass to avoid silting up of the pond.

downstream. Frequently one sees advice to make a silt trap on the upstream side and clear it occasionally, but unless you fancy clearing it out daily in winter it will be utterly futile, since it will most likely fill up the first time the stream is in spate, and thereafter it will be useless. Ideally, cut off the stream flow completely in winter at point A, and only divert sufficient water to maintain pond level in summer. A permanent through flow is not necessary.

BUDGET

If you're planning a tiny or small pond, the budget is probably not the most important factor, but as the size increases and the range of variables expands, it is most definitely worth establishing what it will all cost before you start. It's very tempting to make the pond as large as you can, but then as the costs mount up there is a real risk that compromises will be made at the end, leading to an unsatisfactory result. As a result of internet competition, many of the materials that you will need are similarly priced from many sources and can be costed with great accuracy. At the time of writing, a good quality pond liner costs in the region of £8 per square metre and top-quality underlay about half of that, so the two main ingredients needed for most garden ponds together cost £12 per square metre. A typical garden pond 60cm deep and measuring 4m by 2.5m can therefore be lined for around £300. It will quite likely cost you more to get rid of the unwanted subsoil than to buy the liner and underlay, so to my mind it simply isn't worth trying to reduce that modest

cost by using lower quality materials. The internet forums are full of cheapskate fools using builders' plastic and old carpet, but this approach can easily lead to disappointment. If you're going to do it, better to do it once and do it properly. More detailed information will be found in later chapters.

WHO WILL DO THE JOB?

The next thing you are going to have to decide is whether you aim to complete the job yourself, or with help, or whether you are going to get someone else to do it for you. This is probably the single most important decision you will make in the course of the project, and it is important to get it right. Again, for tiny or small ponds there is little doubt that you will have a good idea of what you want and how you wish to go about it and will probably do it all yourself. A fit person can easily dig out a cubic metre or two of soil in a day by hand in average soil conditions, but if there are old tree stumps to remove or if the ground conditions are challenging it is very hard work indeed. Why not invite some friends around; with sufficient beer and barbecue sausages on hand it is surprising what can be done. Beyond a certain point it is likely that you will be considering using powered machinery such as a mini digger, in which case you need to work out how to get it to where it is needed and how you will move the soil being excavated. Small machines that can access back gardens via a gate or doorway have a very limited reach, so the digging must be carefully planned to avoid 'painting yourself into a corner'. Mini diggers can be hired with or without an operator, and if you have not used one before I strongly recommend that you do the former. Achieving a professional result is not at all easy the first time, especially on a sloping site.

Larger projects

It is perfectly possible to move mountains with hand tools and a great deal of time and effort, but for larger ponds, machinery is a must in most cases. In more restricted locations a mini excavator and wheeled or tracked power barrow or dumper is the most likely combination, but for larger and more accessible sites sometimes a wheeled digger is more versatile. Many operators are used to working mainly on construction sites in a sea of mud and may not appreciate that you

Heavy liners need a big machine to handle them.

don't want your garden to look like the Somme, so it's really important to establish whether your chosen contractor has carried out such work before, and to visit and speak to a recent customer to find out if their experience was good.

If you are going to be using a geotextile liner, then you may need a much bigger machine to handle the heavy rolls than you actually need for the excavation. It is vital if you are using any kind of contractor that you create a proper detailed specification, with sections and plans and a clear explanation of who is to do what. Make absolutely sure that they understand the edge detailing, as this is critical, and so often the one thing that lets down an otherwise well-executed plan.

The gold-plated solution is to employ a pond services company who specialise in this kind of work. If they have been in business for some time, they will have come across all the problems before and will have well-rehearsed solutions. The whole job may even cost less in the end due to their specialist sourcing knowledge and the avoidance of expensive mistakes.

LINER AND WATER-PROOFING OPTIONS

In theory there are many possible lining solutions, but generally these will be determined by the size of the pond. All have their advantages and disadvantages, but the size of the pond will eliminate or favour certain solutions. Liners can be 'passive', which means that

Employing contractors

Do vet the operator carefully before taking them on, since all some machine drivers want to do is to dig as deep as possible, as steep as possible and as quickly as possible. You need to have someone who is going to listen to what you want, take it slowly and steadily, and not over-dig or get carried away. Edge profiling is absolutely critical, and I will return to this topic many times. Once soil has been excavated it is extremely difficult, if not impossible, to put it back without risking it slumping or crumbling afterwards, so as you get close to the required depth and profile it is often a good idea to revert to hand tools to get it just right. Once the digger driver starts work, don't leave them for a second, and if you have to leave even briefly, insist that they stop work until you get back. Don't say I didn't warn you!

they are guaranteed to work straight out of the box, or 'active', relying on a hydration process to work.

The most commonly used liners are:

- Rigid preformed plastic or GRP (glass reinforced plastic or fibreglass) liners.
- Flexible membranes of reinforced polyethylene (RPE), PVC, butyl rubber or EPDM (Ethylene, Propylene, Diene Monomer) rubber.
- Concrete or masonry, often rendered with sand and cement and sealed with one or more coats of a liquid sealant such as G4 or glass reinforced plastic (GRP).
- Puddled or compacted clay layers with or without added bentonite granules.
- Geosynthetic clay liners (GCLs): these comprise multiple fabric layers incorporating bentonite clay, and subsequently covered with a lightly compacted layer of soil; the liner expands on contact with water and forms a seal that is to some extent self-healing.

For very small ponds there will usually be a straight choice between a rigid preformed liner or vessel and a rubber or plastic sheet liner.

Rigid preformed liners

Rigid preformed liners made from plastic or fibreglass (GRP) are widely available, but many suffer from a lack of suitably sized and positioned planting

Pre-formed pond liners frequently have pathetic shelves.

shelves. The larger sizes are relatively expensive and unwieldy to handle. They are also quite tricky to install neatly and require a lot of careful hole sculpting and sand infill to make them level and solid. Small sizes are not as easy to use for raised ponds since the edges are insufficiently strong to support them when full; they must be evenly supported over the whole outer surface. They don't have any overriding advantages but could be a good choice for very small ponds.

Sheet type liners

Sheet type liners can be made in a variety of materials listed previously, and are extremely versatile, being the de facto choice for most garden ponds. Pre-packed and off the shelf liners tend to go up to 10m width and a standard full roll is 30m long. Widths tend to increase in increments of 0.6m, so there is no need to have too much waste. Allow an extra 15–30cm all round to facilitate installation; more than this is likely to be wasted. Larger sizes to about 60 x 30m can be made to order, but larger liners than that must be welded on site.

Cheaper liners are available in various recipes and thicknesses of polyethylene and PVC, some reinforced with fibres and some not; unsurprisingly, you get what you pay for. They are frequently guaranteed for a certain number of years, often fifteen, so they are perfectly adequate in most cases. Builders' plastic is unsuitable, ever, as it will very soon crack and split when exposed to the sun. So, if your budget is restricted (and whose isn't?) or know that for some reason your pond will have a limited lifespan, the less expensive liners can be a valid option. In terms of cost saving alone though, it's hard to justify, given that the cost of a top-quality liner is still only a small fraction of the cost of the completed job. Sheet liners are therefore affordable, easy to handle and can be installed by anyone with half a brain who is prepared to take a little care.

EPDM rubber and butyl rubber

The most popular choice at the time of writing is EPDM rubber. This is a similar material to that used for tyre inner tubes: it is tough, flexible and versatile and well worth the premium price. Butyl rubber is slightly softer, stretchier and more flexible; EPDM is tougher but folds less well. They both come in several thicknesses, most commonly 0.75mm and 1mm, and the bigger the pond the more I would be inclined to go for the heavier grade. They both come with a lifetime guarantee, but this guarantee is against manufacturing defects and deterioration in sunlight, not against some fool with a sharp stone jammed in the cleats of their wellies, or wielding a garden fork with gusto, so bear that in mind when choosing, especially if you are considering one of the cheaper, thinner grades.

Underlay

All types of liner require a spun or woven underlay to protect the liner against sharp objects underneath. It is definitely worth investing in a good quality underlay rather than using old carpet or cardboard, or a sand layer. It's very tempting to economise here, as a good underlay can cost nearly half as much as the liner, but please resist! All the alternatives are easily displaced when installing the liner, they may conceal sharp objects such as staples, and will rot and compact in time, thereafter offering little protection.

Concrete

Before the advent of modern liners, concrete used to be a popular material, and this is still sometimes used in natural swimming ponds, fishponds with vertical sides and certain formal water features. A concrete block shell is often combined with a plastic or rubber liner to act as the waterproofing layer, especially for natural swimming pools. Some ponds are truly epic and require a lot of concrete! However, using concrete on its own has a lot of drawbacks, including the cost, difficulty of waterproofing satisfactorily and the hard work involved in construction. If you're constructing a rectangular pond primarily as a fishpond, it's a good way to go, but for a multi-level pond with shelves and gentle slopes, concrete is not really a sensible choice, and it won't be covered in detail here. Concrete is, however, unavoidable entirely if your pond will be surrounded by paving, since there will need to be a firm hard base at the edges on which to lay the slabs. Concrete pads will also be necessary under the liner to provide support for piers, heavy fountains or statues within the pond.

Large swimming ponds require a lot of concrete and steel.

Clay-lined ponds

In the days before the advent of manufactured liners, most new ponds were waterproofed with a layer of clay. The traditional way to do this was to strip off all topsoil and remove all traces of tree roots, keeping any clay subsoil separate, and then spread clay back into the pond in a layer at least 30cm thick. The area around the pond was then fenced and root crops such as mangelwurzels or turnips scattered about, and sheep or cattle driven into the enclosure. The animals were left in the area long enough to tread and dung on the area until the clay was 'puddled' into an impermeable homogenous and waterproof mass.

Today, in cases where the subsoil contains a sufficiently high percentage of clay, it is possible to compact this in layers to achieve an impermeable result, but often the clay is localised and/or in thin layers and insufficient to do a good job. The traditional tool to use is said to be a sheepsfoot roller; I don't know whether these are mythical, but I have never seen one! Doubtless other more ordinary rollers can be used, and modern tracked excavators do a perfectly good job. A layer of pure bentonite clay, or bentonite mixed with the existing subsoil, can be used to achieve a waterproof layer where natural clay is in short supply. While this can be successful, I would advise against this approach, since if it proves not to be completely waterproof, none of the cost can be recovered and it will then be necessary to resort to a GCL or EPDM liner as well. It is also very labour intensive. If insufficient bentonite has been added to the existing subsoil, or if the layer is not thick enough, or if a small area has been missed or washed out during

application, it will leak, and it will be next to impossible to find the leak.

If the pond lies in a valley or natural crease in the landscape and it is intended to retain the water by means of a dam, it is very important to clear all topsoil and roots from the line of the dam and dig a key trench along the midline of the dam to integrate with the clay layer beneath. This clay barrier is then extended upwards as the dam is built, keeping the best clay for this purpose and enabling the poorer grades to be used for the bulk of the dam both inside and outside. If this is not done correctly, the pressure of water will force it through any weak areas where roots and organic material have decayed, causing a leak which can rapidly become serious.

Building a waterproof dam

Firstly, strip topsoil from the whole area occupied by the pond and dam. Dig a trench in the midline of the dam and fill this with the best clay found while digging out the contours of the pond. Continue to add to this clay core with the best material as the dam is built. Finally spread a layer of topsoil back on the planting shelves and outer slope of the dam. For ponds on a garden scale, these principles apply without a serious risk of disaster.

Note: Building a sizeable dam is an engineering operation and should not be attempted by amateurs; various statutory consents are required.

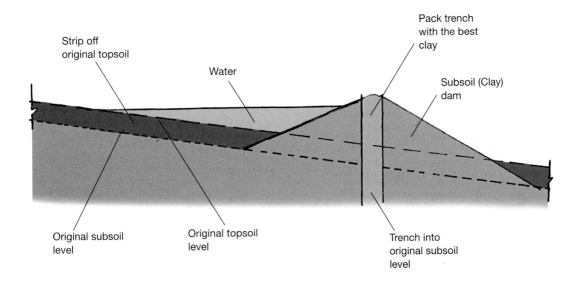

Building a waterproof dam.

Geosynthetic clay liners (GCLs)

Larger ponds, over 10m across the shortest dimension, while they can be lined with a welded rubber liner, are almost invariably lined with clay or a GCL. The full method for application of GCL liners will be detailed in Chapter 4.

Preventing leaks

Along with every lined pond comes the possibility of leaks. These are most often caused by physical damage by something sharp or heavy, but also could result from questing roots both from plants inside and outside the pond. Certain plants have sharp root or shoot tips (mostly the latter) which are capable of puncturing a flexible liner. Phese include *Carex*, *Cyperus*, *Lythrum* and *Typha* genera but are not confined to these. Most shoots turn upwards and are unlikely to penetrate the liner. Perhaps the greatest risk is from horizontal spreading roots or shoots which could travel into a fold in a flexible liner and keep going, but with *Lythrum* it is the sharp woody roots driving straight down that could be problematic. Plants

Some plants have sharp shoots like this Phragmites.

growing inwards from outside such as bamboo or trees and shrubs can cause the same issues. My view is that if a good quality liner is used then the risk is generally overestimated, but as a precaution, it's always best to stand baskets containing such plants on a piece of paving slab or slate and check them regularly to prune off any wayward stems. If support posts for a jetty, heavy statuary or fountains are to be placed within the pond, it's necessary to provide a concrete pad below the liner, sandwiched with an extra layer of spun or woven geotextile either side of the liner to provide padding. In natural swimming ponds, where the liner is covered with a deep layer of shingle into which plants are planted directly, it is normal practice to use a layer of underlay or geotextile both above and below the liner (*see* Chapter 4).

GCLs are self-healing to a point, and small leaks, once located, can theoretically be blocked by adding more clay and/or bentonite around the leak. However, if anything it is harder to locate leaks with a GCL system, given that the leak will be covered by a deep layer of soil. One fact not often appreciated is that bentonite GCLs rely on the weight of the covering soil layer to confine the bentonite. It works by expanding into a fixed volume and hence sealing it, but if there is no confinement or counter-pressure then it will seal poorly if at all. Bentonite powder sprinkled on the top surface is highly unlikely to be successful in sealing a leak in the longer term.

To summarise, for very small ponds, a preformed pond, container or a liner is the most obvious choice; for small to medium-sized garden ponds a flexible liner

Sealing the overlaps with granular bentonite clay.

is most versatile, and for large to very large ponds the choice will be between a rubber-based liner and a GCL.

EDGE PROFILING

A properly constructed edge detail is absolutely vital for the success of your pond and will save you a myriad of maintenance problems. The purpose of a carefully thought-out edge profile is to ensure that none of the liner can be seen once the pond is filled and enable a seamless connection to its surroundings. So often, people get carried away by the excitement of getting on with the job and the result is acres of ugly black plastic visible above water level and narrow sloping shelves on which it is next to impossible to stand baskets of plants. With a little careful planning and attention to detail, this is a simple issue to avoid, but once mistakes are made, they are next to impossible to fix without starting all over again. The key thing to remember is that you need a wide, flat and shallow shelf around a significant proportion of the perimeter for the greatest planting opportunities.

The simplest edge detail of all is to secure the edge of the liner just above water level with turf or flat stones laid directly on the soil. For small or temporary ponds this solution is quick and adequate, provided that the site is level and care has been taken to expose the minimum amount of liner above water level. This method is, however, prone to several problems. Soil is easily washed into the pond from the surrounding area, enriching it and making it murky. The weight of a

Liner retained by flat stones laid on top.

This method exposes the liner and looks unattractive.

shallow layer of soil or turf may also be inadequate to stop the liner from being displaced when standing on the marginal shelf or getting in and out of the pond, the risk being that it is dragged out and the edge dips below water level.

Frequently one sees the liner edge retained flat on the surrounding soil or turf by a loosely-laid row of stones, sometimes infilled with gravel. Stones or slabs laid unevenly like this at the edge of the pond are a safety risk and the whole effect is underwhelming. If the banks of the pond rise significantly above water level at any point, the situation is exacerbated. There is no satisfactory way to fix the edge of the liner against a sloping wall of soil; landscape pegs may seem to be the answer, but it's not really possible to make a tidy job like this. If the liner is exposed right up the bank

Liner retained by turf at the edges.

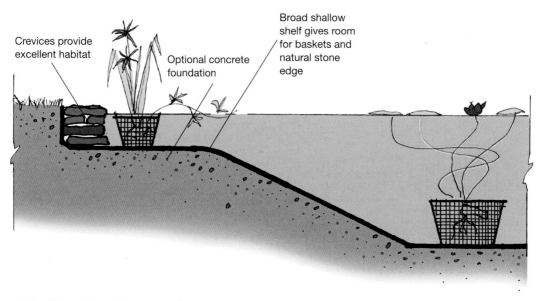

Crevices provide excellent habitat

Optional concrete foundation

Broad shallow shelf gives room for baskets and natural stone edge

Liner retained by an internal dry stone wall.

and over the top, it will look unattractive. Nothing will grow over the area of liner above water level because its foliage will be fried off by the sun in summertime and a significant area of liner will be visible. If you are faced with a fait accompli and this is what you have to deal with, a compromise that can be made is to cut diamond-shaped holes in the exposed part of the liner above water level and plant something tough and creeping through the holes with the aim of covering the remaining network of liner, which will be sufficient to anchor the underwater portion. *Cotoneaster horizontalis* is one such possibility, but this is a bodge, and a re-design is the most sensible option.

Much better is to create a naturalistic edge by using flattish stones laid within the pond and against the outer wall of a wide marginal shelf, leaving sufficient room on the shelf to stand baskets of plants. Use leftover offcuts of liner or underlay under the first layer of stones to give additional protection to the liner beneath, and preferably provide a concrete foundation beneath. The crevices between the stones are excellent places for invertebrates to hide in and provide small planting niches in which creeping plants can get established. Broad, shallow shelves will enable plenty of planted baskets to be stood on them. This in turn

enables small critters to get in and out of the pond safely. If your budget doesn't run to buying natural stone, a reasonably attractive effect can be obtained by using old broken paving slabs, stacked so that the broken edges face outwards into the pond. The rough broken edges soon get covered in algae and allow the roots of creeping plants to get a foothold, the whole looking very natural after a short while. Old paving slabs will leach little lime into the water, so should not

This wildlife pond has broad shelves and dry stone surround providing a lot of hiding places.

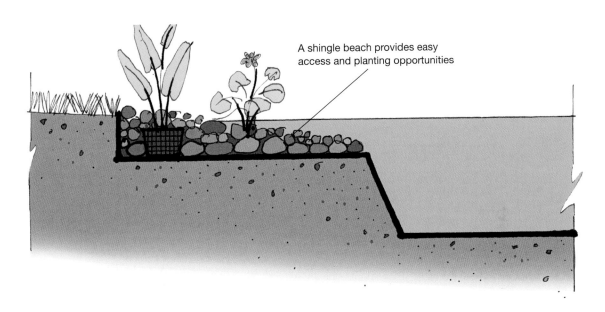

A shingle beach provides easy access and planting opportunities

Shingle beach at one end.

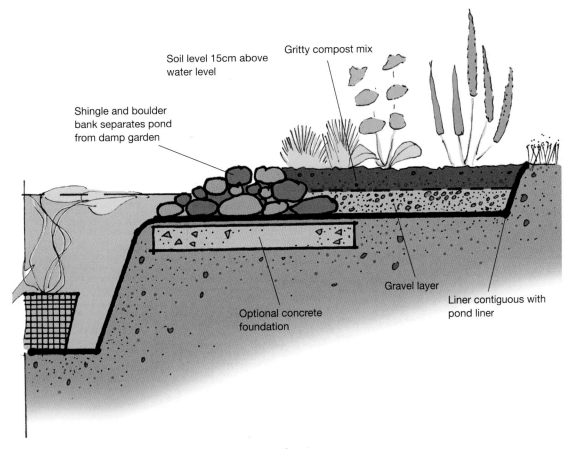

Soil level 15cm above water level

Gritty compost mix

Shingle and boulder bank separates pond from damp garden

Gravel layer

Liner contiguous with pond liner

Optional concrete foundation

This shingle beach separates the pond from the damp garden.

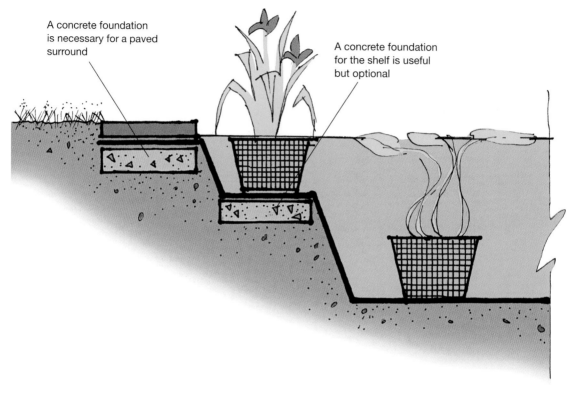

A concrete foundation is necessary for a paved surround

A concrete foundation for the shelf is useful but optional

A concrete foundation is required for hard external landscaping.

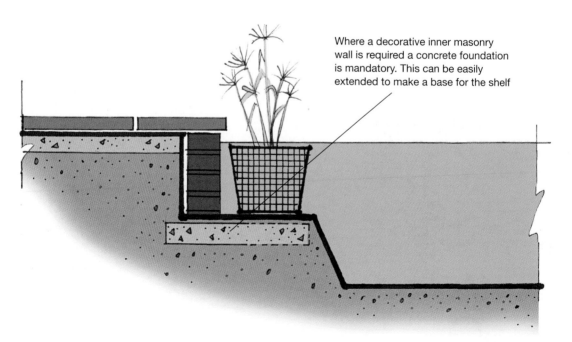

Where a decorative inner masonry wall is required a concrete foundation is mandatory. This can be easily extended to make a base for the shelf

Internal decorative wall and foundation.

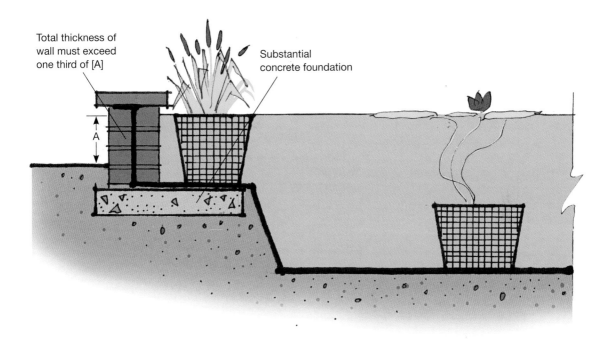

Total thickness of wall must exceed one third of [A]

Substantial concrete foundation

Partially raised pond.

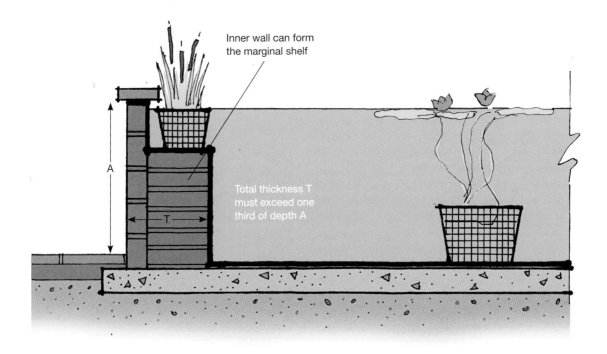

Inner wall can form the marginal shelf

Total thickness T must exceed one third of depth A

Fully raised pond.

cause any problems in this respect. It's not essential to make a concrete foundation strip under the marginal shelf in this instance, unless you plan to mortar the joints between the edging stones for some reason, but it does save a lot of headaches. Not only does it eliminate the risk of the liner becoming stretched over something sharp as it settles (and it will!) but it also stops the inner edge of the shelf from breaking away as people climb in and out of the pond during construction or maintenance.

At some point around the perimeter, you might like to consider the incorporation of a shingle beach. This is a great way to separate a damp garden from the pond itself or enable easy access to the deeper part of the pond. The beach can be partly planted to make it look more natural, and plants such as water spearmint (*Mentha cervina*) are very useful here, releasing a wonderful aromatic scent when trodden on. The beach also enables easy access to the pond by all the critters that use it.

If part, or all, of the pond will be surrounded by hard landscaping such as paving or decking, this will need a concrete edge foundation on which to lay the chosen material, trapping the liner underneath in a bed of mortar. This technique can also be used if you wish to build an internal decorative wall.

For safety or design reasons, you may plan to build a partially or fully raised pond. This solution is certainly a safer bet if there are small children to consider, but remember that any wildlife will find it difficult to get in or out of the pond. In order to build a raised pond, you will need to use a substantial concrete foundation for the perimeter walls, and these walls need to be at least one third as thick as the depth of water retained. Since most people use concrete blocks or bricks for the hidden part of such a build, one can think in terms of their dimensions. A single leaf of concrete block on edge or brick laid flat, being 10cm thick, can retain 30cm of water. A double wall of blocks, or single wall laid flat, or brick laid lengthwise (215mm thickness) can support 60cm of water. For depths over 60cm you would need to use blocks laid double or end on (450mm thickness) which gives support up to 135cm of water. Any facing stone wall can form part of this thickness provided that it is properly tied in to the backing wall. Railway sleepers, or timber of similar hefty dimensions, is another popular choice for a raised pond, and it is easy and quick to create a retaining wall in this way. However, without using an additional, lower wall inside it is difficult to create planting shelves and the timber may be short lived when buried in a damp environment.

GENERAL SAFETY CONSIDERATIONS

Ponds are intrinsically a potential safety hazard, especially to small children and animals, so please consider these carefully. Ponds can be a terrifically educational and enjoyable feature for children, but it is important to encourage a safety-first approach. A broad shallow area or beach will help any unfortunate animal to climb

Slippery slopes of liner invite accidents.

Where tractors are providing regular perimeter maintenance, the top of any bank must be wide enough for safety.

For maximum safety the pond can be completely fenced off.

area surrounding the pond is likely to be maintained using a tractor or powered mower, ensure that the banks are level and broad enough to be safely negotiated. Electrical installations for pumps or lighting should be professionally installed and wired to an appropriate circuit breaker. Any timber posts, jetties, piers or decking should be regularly inspected for safety and replaced or removed if there is any doubt about their integrity. If small children are likely to be unsupervised in the area of the pond, good fencing and a locked gate is the only safe option, but much better is to ensure that they are *always* supervised.

FISH AND DUCKS

out. Poorly planned edges with areas of slippery liner invite accidents. Ensure that surrounding paving is firmly mortared in place and that there are no trip hazards such as hoses or pipes close to the pond. If the

If you intend to keep either of these in your pond, there may be considerable drawbacks as far as planting is concerned. Small, mostly surface feeding fish such as goldfish, sarasas and shubunkins are not a

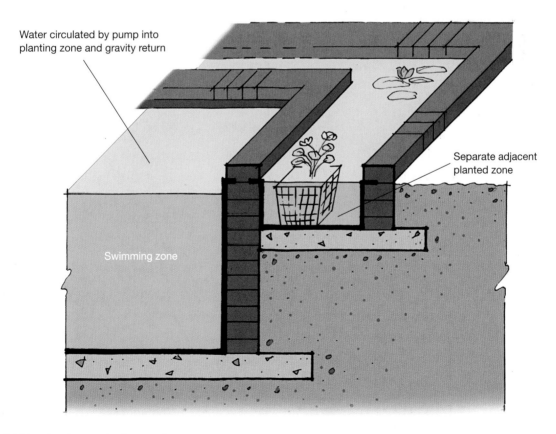

Water circulated by pump into planting zone and gravity return

Separate adjacent planted zone

Swimming zone

Additional perimeter planting trough.

Duck pond, with ducks.

The same pond without ducks.

big problem unless the pond becomes over-stocked with them. Shoaling mid-water and surface feeding fish such as orfe, roach and rudd are also unlikely to cause issues with plants. It is the larger bottom feeding ones such as ordinary carp and koi carp that can be very destructive, especially as they grow to a larger size. The biggest problem derives from feeding fish on an artificial diet, which introduces large quantities of nutrients into the system. Even with a good biological filter, the end result is lots of dissolved nitrates and phosphates which encourage the growth of unwanted algae. While carp or koi measure less than about 25cm long they don't damage plants much, except softer submerged plants such as oxygenators, but as they grow over 30cm, all they want to do is dig, forage in and suck at any green material they can find. They are especially fond of softer foliage and floating plants and leaves; if you float a lettuce in a pond full of carp you will see how quickly they devour it. It does them good, this is part of their natural diet, but it won't do your planting much good. It's all a question of degree, but if sizeable fish are envisaged it may not be possible to include submerged oxygenators, floating or rafting plants in the main pond. Even water lilies can be slowly pestered to death. In a natural earth-bottomed pond one can always tell if there are many carp as the water will be constantly murky due to their constant disturbance of the sediment. Oxygenators will be absent and only the toughest well-established lilies will survive. (Tench don't seem to be troublemakers.)

The best way to include planting with a koi pond is to construct a separate adjacent trough along one or more sides of the pond, and plant into that, giving the illusion that the plants are part of the same pond. Better still is to construct an adjacent filtration bed, planted heavily, through which the pond water flows but into which the fish have no access. In this way you can benefit from the filtration and water treatment provided by the plants as well as the more natural look. This is the same solution as that employed in many natural swimming ponds.

Ducks (and I struggle to even type the word) are even more destructive, since they can attack the marginal plants too. Anything that isn't eaten will be bent, broken or trampled into the mud. You may be delighted when Mrs Mallard arrives with her tiny fluffy chicks, but your smile is apt to disappear when all your plants have been trashed, your pond is a green and brown soup, and your lawn is a sea of mud and poo. Canada geese are the storm troopers of the bird world and in larger ponds and lakes, especially those with islands, they are a complete menace. Accordingly, I always advise that larger ponds should not include islands, as they invariably attract nesting geese. If islands and/or resident geese are present, it's best to plant in autumn, cutting the plants back hard to remove any attractive green foliage to deter any interest, but this may not be enough and temporary fencing or netting may be required to get the plants established. Tougher ones like *Carex*, *Juncus* and *Phragmites* will be fine once they are rooted, but smaller, softer plants stand little chance against geese.

CHAPTER 2

TINY AND SMALL GARDEN PONDS

DISADVANTAGES OF VERY SMALL PONDS

Very small ponds, especially those based on small containers, bring significant challenges and disadvantages. Media reports and well-intentioned articles have encouraged many to consider that any container of water in the garden will provide wildlife benefits, but this needs to be qualified with a number of caveats. The last thing that anybody sets out to do is to install a death trap in their garden, but unfortunately an old washing up

Some improvements are still necessary for this installation.

bowl full of water is likely to become just that. Amphibians will spawn just about anywhere wet, and if the vessel of water dries out before their eggs or tadpoles develop legs, it's the end for them all. The same applies to eggs and larvae of any insects too. Small animals like voles and hedgehogs can easily drown in small, steep-sided containers too. So, if you are planning a very small water volume, it's important to site it well and keep it topped up with water, with the brim only just above ground level and some plant or other material bridging the gap from water to land. Small, planted containers can dry out in just a day or two in hot weather, so it's a good idea to site them somewhere that they will be seen daily. As ever, a little care taken during installation will ensure that your pond adds to, rather than detracts from your garden. In the previous example, a rather hasty approach has led to a lacklustre result. All the right elements are present, but the planting is a little underwhelming and the loose bricks at the edge need to be set into some cement for safety. Some external planting could link the pond to the rest of the garden border.

SMALL POND OPTIONS

A large range of preformed pond liners can be found at larger garden centres and aquatic centres; these vary widely in quality, price and design, but some more

Small patio pond.

Semi-formal wildlife pond.

Timber-edged pond.

exact requirements in terms of size and shape. Timber is a relatively cheap and versatile material and can be used with a liner for smaller ponds. However, with imagination a whole range of re-purposed containers can be used, as long as you remember their limitations.

Vessels that are deep relative to their width or length, like half barrels, cattle troughs, baths or old water tanks, will be awkward to plant, since small plants need very shallow water. There are some solutions to this, either partly filling the container with inert material such as stones, gravel or sand, or providing some kind of stable shelf or deep planting basket inside. Don't put soil inside to build up the level, or the result will be a green slimy mess. Nor should you use new concrete blocks, as they will raise the pH too high. Weathered and/or washed materials are best. The best format from the wildlife point of view is a shallow and wide one, the main downside being that it will tend to dry out more rapidly in hot or dry weather. Regarding the position, smaller ponds are best somewhere that is bright but not in full sun during the hottest part of the day. They should be away from sources of windblown leaves, since a significant quantity of decaying leaves in a small water volume will produce an acidic, anaerobic

recent designs do incorporate shelves or channels for planting. As we have seen in Chapter 1, some off-the-shelf preformed ponds are next to useless, and aren't particularly easy to install either, so many people choose to make their own, or use a range of recycled materials. The old favourite of a hole with a liner is a common option, and this means that you can tailor it to your

Galvanised trough pond.

and probably poisonous soup. It's best if the container is at least partially sunk into the ground, which will reduce the temperature variation and make it easier for critters to get in and out. A freestanding steep-sided container is of little use to wildlife.

SAFETY CONSIDERATIONS

It's tempting to ignore safety when designing and installing a very small pond, but accidents can and do still happen, even with very shallow water. Where very small children are concerned the outcome can be unthinkable, so take care to consider this fully. Babies and toddlers should be completely excluded from the pond area by fencing, and steep slopes with water at the bottom should be avoided. There should be no possible way for an older child to bang their head and fall into water. Surfaces around the pond should be non-slip; timber is the worst – a pond recessed into timber decking would be an extreme example, but any hard surfaces can soon become slippery with algae. Any perimeter walling should not encourage or allow a child to walk along or balance on the top. Stepping stones, piers and jetties are extremely hazardous. Raised ponds are intrinsically safer provided that it is not possible for a child to clamber or fall in.

PLANTING IN SMALL PONDS

For a small pond it's important to choose appropriate plants. One needs plants which have a long season of interest, are not too vigorous or tall (though a single tall architectural resident is a possibility) and preferably native. That's actually a pretty short list, and might include *Juncus ensifolius* and *Veronica beccabunga*, together with oxygenators such as *Callitriche* (starwort) or *Ceratophyllum* (hornwort). Many like to have a tiny water lily in their mini-pond, but pygmy lilies are rarely suitable as they don't cope with much competition and need full sun and clear water. If you do fancy one, a small type lily is often best (*see* Chapter 8). Please remember that if the water volume is small, it will need topping up frequently in hot or dry weather, probably every day, so if this just isn't going to happen, consider making a bigger pond with more stable conditions or choose a water feature with no standing water instead.

The smaller the pond, the greater percentage of the surface needs to be covered by plants, perhaps as much as 90 per cent for tiny ones, reducing to 50 per cent in ponds over 10m².

PLANTS FOR SMALL PONDS

The following plants are suitable for use in smaller ponds as they aren't too tall or vigorous.

(Native plants in bold type.)

Acorus gramineus cvs (Japanese sweet flag)
***Anagallis tenella* (bog pimpernel)**
Anemopsis californica (yerba mansa)
***Baldellia ranunculoides* (lesser water plantain)**
***Caltha palustris* (marsh marigold)**
***Cardamine pratensis* (lady's smock)**
Carex muskingumensis 'Little Midge' (palm sedge)
***Carex panicea* (carnation grass)**
***Ceratophyllum* (hornwort)**
Cotula coronopifolia (golden buttons)
***Eleocharis acicularis* (needle spike-rush)**
***Eriophorum vaginatum* (hare's tail cotton grass)**
Gunnera magellanica
***Hydrocharis morsus-ranae* (frogbit)**

Hydrocotyle spp. (small cvs)
Isolepsis cernua (fibre optic grass)
Juncus ensifolius (flying hedgehogs)
Justicia americana (water willow)
Lobelia chinensis (water lobelia)
Luronium natans (floating water plantain)
Lychnis flos-cuculi (ragged robin)
Lysimachia nummularia (creeping Jenny)
Mentha cervina (water spearmint)
Persicaria amphibia (amphibious bistort)
Phyla lanceolata (frog fruit)
Ranunculus flammula (lesser spearwort)
Sagittaria sagittifolia (arrowhead)
Veronica beccabunga (brooklime)

Small planted container feature.

A few more suggestions for mini ponds

Aquarium-type feature pond.

Bowl-based mini pond.

Example of a tiny pond installation

The site for this mini pond was chosen because the wall faces south-east, providing morning sun but getting shadier in the hottest part of the day. It's also close to the back door of the house, so will be seen daily to avoid the risk of it becoming dried out without being noticed. The overgrown wall climbers were cut back and the motley collection of poorly performing plants in the border removed. The old earthenware sink was found at a farm sale and was buried in the ground to two thirds its depth. This helps to prevent too much soil and windblown rubbish from falling directly into it without forming too much of a barrier to creatures getting in and out. To my mind, this size of mini pond is about the smallest that is viable. A small beach of cobbles and pebbles was placed at one end to allow creatures access.

A few selected plants were then placed inside; these include *Juncus ensifolius* for a little height and evergreen foliage; *Isolepsis cernua* for a long season display; *Veronica beccabunga* and *Lysimachia nummularia* which will root both inside and outside the pond to link the two environments and camouflage the edges; one *Caltha palustris* for early and late colour and *Hippuris vulgaris* and a couple of bunches of *Ceratophyllum* for oxygenation.

A few shorter cannas were spare in the greenhouse, so they were used as a temporary late display to the rear; these will be removed in late autumn and replaced with small hostas to give a long season of foliage interest at the back. A handful of *Lychnis* 'White Robin' help to lift the display with their starry white flowers.

After a while the *Lysimachia* and *Veronica* will spread well beyond the sides of the pond and provide ground cover all around it. Little open water is exposed, and this will help to reduce evaporation. I was delighted to see that within five minutes of finishing, a dragonfly had perched just above the pond in the cut back wall climber to check it out.

Site for tiny pond.

Old earthenware sink.

Small pebble beach enables access.

Water plants installed.

Planting completed.

CHAPTER 3

MEDIUM AND LARGE GARDEN PONDS

I hope that by now I have convinced you to make your pond a little larger than the minimum. When planning slightly larger ponds, the principles remain the same but there are many more opportunities to make the pond more visually interesting as well as attractive to wildlife. Rather than a single planting depth, it will be possible to create more shelves to suit different groups of water plants, increasing the number of niches in which creatures can dwell. However, the most valuable area is always the shallowest shelf around the edges, and it is better to have one wide, flat shelf here than two or three narrow ones at different depths. For a pond of about 6m², aim for half to be occupied by the shallow marginal shelf and half to be the full depth. There is absolutely no need or advantage to making the pond deeper than 70 to 90cm at its deepest either. The deeper you go, the more of the pond area will be taken up by the unplantable sloping sides, so it's much better to have a single wide shelf at 15–20cm deep, supporting planted baskets of about the same depth, and a large flat base on which baskets of water lilies, oxygenators and other deep-water plants can be placed.

If your pond is intended for wildlife and amenity, and fish are not envisaged, there will be no need for filters, pumps, aerators or any of that jazz. The plants will do all this for you, but they won't do it instantly, especially if you are miserly with your planting. The key aim for clear water is to cover 50–70 per cent of the water surface with plants, and the smaller the pond, the higher this percentage should be. In deeper water, this can be achieved with rafting plants growing inwards from the edges, or those with floating leaves, or free-floating plants. This is very hard to achieve from the get-go and is a constant source of angst for new pond keepers. Algae are the fastest growing plants on the planet, so they will get started long before the bigger and more complex plants have had a chance to create the required cover. You will need to be relaxed about this for the first year or more, as your pond goes through a series of algal blooms and infestation with blanket weed, before a natural balance begins to occur, and it will. Try not to micro-manage it and avoid using any of the expensive bottles of gunk that are 'guaranteed' to solve the problem. Remove excess algae manually if necessary (it's not that hard) and give it time. A fine meshed pond net is very handy for this, as is a stiff bristled broom.

Containers for pond plants

The most versatile containers for medium sized ponds will be mesh baskets between 3 and 10 litres in volume. These will normally be 10–20cm deep, and ideally should be placed so that the edge of the basket is just below water level for marginal plants, and at various other depths for deep water plants. Baskets are available in a variety of depths, sizes and shapes to fit any situation. Plants that aren't true marginals, like *Anagallis* and *Lychnis flos-cuculi*, will require baskets to be positioned so that the rim is slightly higher than water level. Detailed planting advice is given in Chapter 9.

A selection of aquatic plant baskets.

Plants of various heights and habits can be used to make a visually interesting, seasonally varied and diverse habitat. The old adage of planting design applies, which is that it is far better to use relatively few different species but multiple plants of the same type in groups, in random patches and with occasional repeats, than to have dozens of different single plants like soldiers in a row. If you buy all the plants at the same time, it is quite likely that you will be seduced by those that look at their best at that time of year. This will result in a display that looks poor at a different time of year, since all those you have chosen will be brown stumps at the same time too. So, do try to consider seasonality before filling all the available space with impulse purchases in one go. More on seasonality in Chapter 5.

LARGE GARDEN PONDS UP TO 100M²

All of the same principles apply as the pond size increases, but if anything, it is even more important to make the right plant choices. If something turns out to be much more invasive than expected, it's not too much of a disaster in a small pond, because if necessary and with a little hard work it can all be hauled out and disposed of and a new start can be made. The paradox with larger ponds is that more vigorous plants may be required to fill all the space, but if one of these gets out of hand it is very difficult to start again without a great deal of work and expense. In the case of a natural pond, or one with a GCL, once the plants have become well established in soil or gravel it can be nigh on impossible to remove them; tiny pieces of rhizome soon regenerate and a massive seed bank in the mud will soon establish and ensure rapid re-colonisation. On the other hand, smaller, more delicate plants can soon become overrun.

Separation gaps

One useful technique is to create separation gaps between blocks of vigorous plants, using deep water between to isolate the groups, but it is very difficult to stop plants with long, strong rhizomes, like *Typha* and *Phragmites*, from spreading sideways in the margins or seeding around. If your conscience permits, the least damaging way to maintain gaps is to spot treat with glyphosate; otherwise resign yourself to a lot of manual pulling and digging. The most invasive plants should be avoided in ponds smaller than 0.5 hectares. These are *Carex acuta*, *Carex acutiformis*, *Carex riparia*, *Glyceria aquatica*, *Phalaris*, *Phragmites*, *Schoenoplectus lacustris*, and *Typha* species except *T. minima*.

CASE STUDY: CONSTRUCTION OF A MEDIUM-SIZED GARDEN POND

Step 1: The grass surrounding the pond has been killed off with a non-persistent spray, since the lawn was in very poor condition anyway. The paving slabs that will form the left-hand edge have been lifted and the perimeter of the pond first marked out with string and then a trench dug to a width of 450mm and a depth of 250mm. Pegs have been installed in the trench to mark a depth of concrete of 100mm. This took one man one day by hand for a pond approximately 5m by 3m.

Step 2: Concrete has been mixed at a ratio of six parts all-in ballast to one part cement and placed in the trench to the top of the pegs, then allowed to cure for two days. This will form the shelf of the pond and is wide enough (500mm) to allow for a natural stone wall and a five-litre pond basket. While the concrete was

Step 2: Concrete now forms the shelf and stabilises the edges.

Step 1: The perimeter of the pond has been dug out to the level of the base of the first shelf.

Step 3: Excavation to full depth is complete.

setting, the excavation of the area to become the damp garden was begun. Subsoil is being tipped in an old badly sited pond at the end of the garden and under trees, while the topsoil and old turf is being retained for use in the damp border later.

Step 3: The remainder of the turf and topsoil has been stripped off down to the level of the concrete and stacked to one side. Excavation of the main body of

Step 4a: A sump for the bottom drain is made.

Step 4b: A trench connects the bottom drain to a filter box.

Step 5: The underlay has been installed and the liner loosely fitted on top.

Step 6: The pond is being filled and the liner carefully pleated. Natural stone is stacked on the shelf to hide the vertical upstand of liner.

the pond down to the full depth has begun; the concrete shelf now forming a hard inner edge to prevent crumbling. The gap in the concrete shelf on the left-hand side is to allow for a connection to a filter box since the client wished to keep koi in this pond. This would not normally be necessary.

Step 4: This step is not necessary if fish are not envisaged, but a bottom sump was created in order to lead debris to a bottom drain and thence to a filter box connected via a pump to a small waterfall in the foreground. The photo for Step 4b shows the connection line to the filter.

Step 5: The hole has been pre-lined with a woven geotextile underlay followed by an EPDM rubber liner which is now loosely pleated. Lots of small pleats are preferable to fewer large ones and will make for a neater result.

Step 6: The pond has been filled slowly while the pleats in the liner were carefully arranged and allowed to settle for a day or two. Pebbles and cobbles were used to separate the damp area at the back from the pond itself and create a beach into the water, and the old turf was stacked upside down at the end to form the damp garden. The finished level of this area is about 150mm above water level. Natural stone was dry stacked around the perimeter to retain the liner against the excavation sides; some offcuts of underlay were used behind and under the first course to give the liner some protection (*see* also Chapter 1). The existing paving was re-set on top of the dry stone wall.

Step 7: The adjacent lawn has been re-turfed, and a small pebble area created to the right-hand side to echo the pebble beach and provide a clean area for access. The pond and damp garden have been planted. The last picture was taken a year later.

A FULLY RAISED RUBBER-LINED POND

In this design, wide shelves are punctuated by large river boulders to give an informal look. Large baskets on the bottom of the pond are supported on piers to extend the planting out into the pond.

Step 7: The perimeter paving has been re-laid and the plants installed.

One year on and the pond looks well established.

Construction of this raised pond is complete.

The raised pond has been planted up.

Four months on and the plants have grown enormously.

Detail of planting.

A SIMPLE LARGE RUBBER-LINED POND

This pond relies on a large amount of natural stone to cover the exposed liner where it has been brought

Another view of the completed planting.

The site for this large informal garden pond has been marked out with a hosepipe.

The bulk of the digging is complete and the soil has been lost in a perimeter bank.

With this technique a great deal of stone is necessary to cover the exposed liner around the edges.

The liner is in and the pebble beach installed.

The pond is complete.

Natural stone is being used around the perimeter.

over a perimeter bank of soil. This is fine where plenty of stone is available, but a more straightforward approach using a wide marginal shelf, as in Chapter 1, would use a lot less stone, which is expensive to purchase.

CHAPTER 4

PONDS ON A LARGER SCALE

Some readers may be planning a pond on a much larger scale, and this brings a fresh set of challenges. It is more of an engineering proposal than a garden or landscape project and specialist advice will be necessary. Statutory consents may be required for various aspects of the operation and may include planning permission, abstraction and discharge consents and/or impoundment licence and a fish stocking licence if fish are envisaged. The Environment Agency is a good place to start, and useful contact details can be found at the end of this book. Projects like this can be truly epic, and if costs are not to spiral out of control a fully detailed and costed proposal must be drawn up.

NATURAL SWIMMING PONDS

This natural swimming pond has a wild feel.

These have become really popular and require a completely different approach to simple garden pools. They are relatively expensive to construct, and it is very tempting to cut corners to control the cost, but such compromises will affect their performance. Such ponds are best installed by professionals, since the construction and control systems are complicated, technical and easy to get wrong. There have been many instances of DIY projects which have proved to

be well beyond the skills of the enthusiastic amateur, leading to disappointment with the result. Simply lining a hole and planting into gravel is not the only requirement for success. In essence, a natural swimming pond uses plants to achieve what chemicals and filtration do in a traditional swimming pool. One major difference is that a traditional swimming pool is biologically sterile and kept that way by application of pool chemicals such as salt and chlorine, but a natural swimming pool contains a complete biological ecosystem. The planted zones can be partially or completely within the same zone as the swimming area or in a separate regeneration zone connected to the swimming zone by pumps and pipes.

Swimming pond theory

The theory requires some fairly sophisticated chemistry outside the scope of this book, but fortunately there is an excellent book on the subject by Kircher and Thon (*see* Suggested Further Reading) which is comprehensive and highly recommended for those with a thirst to know how it works and indeed for anybody planning to install a natural swimming pond.

There are three possible variations on plant positioning fully within the swimming zone; partly in the swimming zone and partly in an external regeneration zone; or wholly in an external regeneration zone. There are also various accepted levels of technicality, described by Kircher and Thon as being:

1. Standing water with no pumped circulation and over 65 per cent planted area
2. Slow-moving water through the planting zone, occupying 50 per cent or more of the area – this is referred to as a Hydrobotanical System (HBS)
3. Moderate flow rate of at least 300 litres per m² per hour through an inert medium constituting >30 per cent of the total area – a Technical Wetland (TWL)
4. Fast-moving flow of >500 litres per m² per hour in a biofilm accumulating substrate (BSF)

Taken together, these three design possibilities and four levels of technicality result in a possible twelve model combinations, though some are not compatible and many real-life installations involve some degree of hybridisation.

OVERVIEW

The space available here permits only a brief overview of the issues, and it's a bit like summarising a Shakespeare play on a single side of A4, but the essential principle is to use plants, growing in an inert medium such as gravel, to take up free nutrients in the water to prevent the growth of algae and keep the water clear. Absolute clarity is not always possible, especially with the less technical systems, since the presence of organic material in the form of plants and primitive animals means that some particles of organic matter are always present, affecting clarity.

The two key nutrient parameters are phosphorus and carbon, but there are many other important parameters, the paradox being that the aquatic plants require sufficient nutrients to survive and grow, but the water must contain very low levels of these minerals to reduce algal growth to an absolute minimum. In areas with medium to high water hardness, phosphorus limitation is easier to achieve than carbon limitation, but in low hardness areas carbon limitation is more of a possibility. The minimum requirement is for a *substantial* degree of planting in a clean substrate such as gravel. DIY ponds frequently do not contain sufficient shallow planted zones or enough plants to achieve the required effect. Typically, a swimming zone at least 2m deep and devoid of plants is surrounded by a shallower planted zone, though it is much easier to maintain the planting if the swimming zone is completely separated from the planted zone so that the latter can be drained for easier access and maintenance without involving the loss of all the water.

With a pumped system, the gravel in which the plants grow allows water to flow upwards or downwards, depending on the design, bringing all the water continuously in contact with the plant roots. One or more pumps or airlifts provide the driving force, and the pumps are usually situated in a separate valved pump chamber. Additional technology such as phosphate stripping chambers or ultraviolet lights are sometimes added, but these disqualify the system from the definition of a natural swimming pond. The swimming zone is kept spotlessly clean by regular vacuuming with a pool vac, and while the water clarity may not always be crystal clear, the aim is to keep it as clear as possible.

SUITABLE PLANTS

The plants which are selected need to conform to certain ideals, such as a clean growth habit (producing little debris and not exploding into balls of fluff in autumn like the pokers of reed mace), and a non-invasive nature coupled with a reasonably strong growth which ensures that plenty of nutrients are taken up. Additionally, they are expected to look good of course, so a long season of interest is beneficial. Since the whole aim is to minimise the dissolved nutrient level, plants are normally purchased bare rooted and planted direct into the gravel medium, though for some, such as water lilies, I recommend that they are introduced as well rooted potted plants to get them started. With well-established plants, the roots should have already absorbed a lot of the nutrients in the soil and locked up the soil around them to prevent it from leaching into the water. All that is necessary is to trim off any roots and mud outside of the basket and plunge the whole thing into the gravel planting medium. The baskets will soon be subsumed, and the lilies will spread well beyond their confines within a couple of years. Alternatively, the whole plant can be carefully knocked out of the pot and gently washed to remove any loose soil before planting. Remember the same principles apply regarding planting depth; too often natural swimming ponds are constructed with a steep bank of shingle leading from the outer edge to the edge of the deep zone, making planting very difficult. This results in very little in the way of shallow water,

The shingle slope here is too steep to plant easily.

The shingle slope here is gentle and easily planted.

which is the only place that many of the most attractive marginal plants will grow, and they will be restricted to a narrow fringe round the outside. Aim to have large areas of just 2–5cm of water over the gravel planting medium for the most versatile planting possibilities.

VERY LARGE PONDS

Once ponds get over a certain size it is almost certain that a contractor will be involved for the excavation and construction. It goes without saying that the best choice will be someone who has carried out this kind of work many times before and is not learning at your expense (*see* Chapter 1). They should be very familiar with all the guidelines below, but as ever, it is useful for the client to know almost as much as the expert.

A healthy lily will have a lot of roots and leaves.

A case study is pictured at the end of this chapter and the basic operation is set out below.

Stage 1: Preparation

You will avoid a lot of stress and argument if you prepare a proper plan and operating guide well before the contractor arrives. Professional operators much prefer a client who knows what they want and gives clear instructions, and this may save you a proportion of the 'fudge factor' that they must build into their quote to cover unexpected problems. Depth contours should be clearly marked. Shelves that are level across their whole width are much easier to plant up than sloping shelves. Take great pains to explain that you don't want the banks at 45 degrees to the vertical (which is what the machine driver will be used to doing on construction sites), and explain the reasons why (have you tried walking up or down a slippery, wet mud bank at 45 degrees?). Slowly and carefully is the brief.

If you don't want to end up with a sea of mud way beyond the pond margins, it's really important to get some stakes and hazard tape and mark off any areas that you want to preserve. You will need to leave adequate room for excavators, dumpers, or tractor and trailer to negotiate safely but if you leave the average dumper driver to his own devices, he will tend to meander all over the place! You can always extend the permitted driving area if there are problems with bogging down. Once the 'no go' areas have been taped off, you will need to mark out the perimeter of the pond with marker spray and install a set of levelling pegs to enable the contours to be accurately followed as the dig progresses. The necessary laser level and sighting pole can be cheaply hired, but if you have never done this before it is probably well worth paying a surveyor for a few hours to do it for you. Keep the levelling pegs well outside the edge of the pond perimeter so they don't get lost when digging out the last bit at the edge.

Stage 2: Excavation

Start the excavation furthest from the tip area, so that you progressively tidy up as you go. Firstly, strip off just the top 5–10cm of turf and soil and stack this in a separate heap. This material will eventually be used around the outside of the pond to tidy up ruts and in any deeper parts of the pond where water lilies will reside. They will benefit from the higher nutrient content, and the turf and weeds will die out if more than 30cm below the water surface. Avoid using it in the shallow areas and margins, as it will be full of turf clods and weed seeds and will make life a misery after planting. Then strip off the rest of the topsoil layer and stack separately too; this soil will be used on the banks to provide a less rich but mostly weed-free medium in which to plant the marginal plants. Do this in the area which will receive the unwanted subsoil too, stacking the topsoil to one side so that you can cover the tip area at the end with the original soil. Lastly, dig out the subsoil to the required depth contours and tip on the pre-prepared tip area. Ensure that the driver does not dig out the banks too steeply (this is a common issue and one which is impossible to fix unless there is the possibility of extending the pond even further. A maximum slope of 1 in 3 should be possible; any steeper than that and it's likely to subside or collapse.

In the case of a geotextile lining system, or compacted clay waterproofing layer, you will need to excavate all the levels at least 30cm below their final finished level, because 30cm of soil is returned over the top of the liner or compacted clay to confine and protect it and provide a planting medium. This is obviously adjustable to an extent, by using more than 30cm of soil, but it's best not to use less, so a wise pond builder will allow for a few centimetres more if required.

These banks have been cut much too steeply and are unplantable and dangerous.

Shelf depths

IMPORTANT: For a GCL covered with soil, or other planting medium, the finished marginal shelf should be 2–10cm below maximum water level. For a rubber liner, shelves must be created to exactly the right level to allow for the depth of the baskets intended, and if it is wrong can only be rectified by using deeper or shallower baskets in which to put the plants. Best to get it right then! In the case of a rubber liner, the shelf will usually need to be 15–20cm below maximum water level, but as much as 30cm if the biggest baskets are used.

Margins in an earth pond.

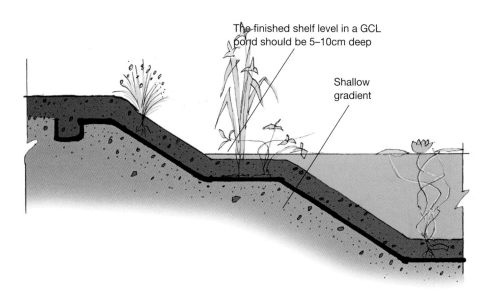

The finished shelf level in a GCL pond should be 5–10cm deep

Shallow gradient

Margins in a rubber-lined pond.

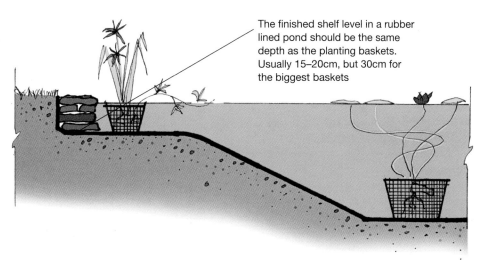

The finished shelf level in a rubber lined pond should be the same depth as the planting baskets. Usually 15–20cm, but 30cm for the biggest baskets

It may be that you need to leave an access ramp at the end closest to the tip site in order for the excavator to get out; the driver can tidy this up on the way out. During the main excavation, try to avoid the situation where the digger needs to replace soil previously excavated, as it will never go back as firm as the undug soil. It's very likely that at some time during the work on larger projects that it will rain, or water will start seeping up from the ground, or you will come across an old land drain that weeps water into the hole. If this starts to happen things can deteriorate very quickly, so it's vital to have a pump on site to remove this, or you will soon be faced with thousands of gallons of slop to deal with and the whole job will grind to a halt. The best advice is to stop work immediately until the water can be dealt with. If the winter water table might be higher than the deepest part of the pond, it is advisable to lay a necklace of land drains under the liner to allow this to run away, or you could well end up with 'hippos' in your pond, where in winter ground water pressure forces the liner upwards in huge bubbles, separating the joints and compromising the water seal, since it rarely all settles back as it was. This is particularly problematic with GCLs, since once the seams have separated or the covering layer of soil loosened or disturbed, the seal will be lost. If there is nowhere on the adjacent land that is lower than the base of the pond, you may need to construct a sump outside the pond to connect to so that groundwater can be pumped out when necessary.

If you are relying on a high clay content in the subsoil to achieve a waterproof layer, it is usually only necessary to get the digger driver to track backwards and forwards over the area to compact it. You will need a layer at least 30cm deep, preferably spread and compacted in two 15cm layers. In some cases, depending on your soil type, you may need up to a metre depth of subsoil to achieve a watertight result if there is a high stone or sand content in the clay. If you had been planning to use a compacted clay seal to waterproof the pond but come across a gravel layer during excavation that is weeping water in, you may need to reconsider. Water pressure from such springs will steadily work on the covering layers and force its way through. It's often simply assumed that these 'springs' will fill the pond and keep it fresh but remember that it can work both ways. If water can come in, it can also leak out, and it will, just

as soon as the water table drops below the spring outlet. You may then end up with an empty pond in summer.

However, given the availability and affordability of modern geotextile liners, these are the most commonly used option.

Stage 3: GCL liner installation

This is a tricky operation and requires a careful and methodical approach. Full instructions can be obtained from the manufacturers, but the gist is this. The standard size of the rolls used is 20m by 5m, and they weigh over a ton each when dry, so you need a large machine to lift a steel centre tube over 5m long which carries the roll. This centre bar does not come with the rolls, so your contractor will have to provide it, along with the chain slings to suspend it. Do not allow the roll of liner to get wet before installation, because they will weigh 13 tons when saturated and become impossible to handle. If access is limited and a large excavator cannot be used, narrower rolls (about 2.5m wide) are also available, but you will then need to allow for the larger number of overlaps. The liner is anchored in a trench above water level and unrolled along the long axis of the pond, unless the measurements make it expedient to lay it crossways. Each roll is overlapped

Handling the heavy rolls of liner needs specialised equipment.

with the previous one, usually by about 30cm, and granular bentonite is poured between the overlaps to help to seal the joint. Once it is in place it's next to impossible to move without damaging it, so take care. Once all the strips have been laid and jointed, the trenches containing the ends are backfilled tightly to secure the ends. It's important now not to drive over the liner until it is covered with a 30cm layer of soil, and preferably not drive on it again at all to avoid the risk of displacing the liner. One fact often not appreciated is that in order for waterproofing to be effective, bentonite liners rely on the weight of the covering soil layer to confine it. Bentonite works by expanding into an enclosed space and hence sealing it, but if there is no confinement or counter-pressure then it will seal poorly.

Sometimes, a rubber-based liner is specified for very large ponds; this can be for a variety of reasons but often it is due to the requirement for a clean swimming pond or lack of access for the large machines needed for the geotextile system. EPDM (Ethylene, Propylene, Diene Monomer) is the most likely material; this is fairly tough and can be manufactured in almost any size. For really large ponds, liners may be welded together on site. Their weight is considerably less than that of geotextile, but large rolls are still extremely heavy and will need a lot of manpower or machines to handle. Installation is a simple matter of unrolling in position, but you do need to start right since the liner will be very difficult to adjust once unrolled. In this case, the edges are secured either in trenches, under hard landscaping detail at the edge or with barbed plastic landscape pegs on a flat shelf above water level. A good quality underlay is essential. Often an additional layer of underlay is used over the top to prevent damage by subsequent cover by shingle.

Stage 4: Returning soil for planting (geotextile or clay-lined ponds only)

Once the liner has been laid and the ends fixed in the backfilled trenches, a layer of soil must be spread and lightly compacted on top to provide a reasonable planting medium. This also applies to ponds using a compacted clay waterproofing layer. For the latter, although some roots may eventually penetrate the clay waterproofing layer, it is best that they don't, as it will compromise the waterproofing, so again the added soil layer should be at least 30cm deep. Ideally, a long reach machine will drop the soil from the outside and lightly tamp it in place with the back of the bucket, but if the size of the pond precludes this and the big machine can't reach the inner areas, most contractors will use a mini digger to spread and lightly compact this layer. The big machine is then sometimes used as a crane to move the small one about, to avoid damaging the liner beneath or compacting the planting layer too heavily by driving all over it.

Planting of very large ponds

Even at this size, there are still some plants which should be used with extreme caution, especially if there are large areas of shallow water. *Phragmites*, *Schoenoplectus* and *Typha* should only be considered if there is deep water in front to restrict their spread, and it may still be necessary to control their lateral spread. Once ponds reach this size they are almost certainly surrounded by wild natural areas, so care should be taken not to introduce plants that might escape and cause problems. A scheme including only native plants is the safest option, but there are a few non-native plants which are highly unlikely to spread beyond the confines of the pond, such as *Acorus* and *Pontederia*, which can be very useful to increase diversity.

Banks leading directly to deep water restrict the outward spread of vigorous plants.

VERY LARGE PONDS OVER 0.5HA (5,000M²)

Ponds and lakes of this size are major engineering works and will require specialists to be employed. Planning permission will almost certainly be required, unless it is a purely agricultural operation, and various geological and wildlife surveys may be necessary. If the amount of water impounded exceeds 25,000m³ there is an additional requirement to obtain an impoundment licence. Since major operations are involved, the Health and Safety Executive must be informed, and a full Health and Safety procedure will need to be drawn up. Ponds of this size can include any native plants and a professionally prepared planting plan will reap dividends. Clearly, large numbers of plants will be required, and it is likely that the supplier will help with selection, especially if consulted at an early stage.

It may seem obvious, but the larger the pond, the more water will be required to fill it and to compensate for summer evaporation and transpiration. Consider whether the amount available, perhaps from roofs, a borehole or a small stream or spring, will be adequate to keep up with the summer demand, and make sure you don't over-size the pond. Ponds which fill only in winter and completely dry again by early summer are of little value, though natural ponds with some drying and exposure provide a rare habitat.

General planting advice for larger ponds

One option promoted by many environmentalists is not to plant anything at all, but to wait for colonisation to occur naturally. This hinges on the basis that since most larger ponds are sited in naturally damp or low-lying areas, there may already be a seed bank in the soil. My problem with this approach is mostly that the timescale is too long, and it will probably be very many years before any kind of diversity is attained. I guess that's okay if your family have owned the land for several generations and your offspring may eventually benefit, but realistically most people want to see a result not just in their lifetime but in pretty short order,

having spent many thousands of pounds creating their dream. My other main criticism with the leave-it-alone philosophy is that the first colonisers will almost always be the vigorous and invasive species that I have been warning about, and once they are well underway with little competition, a monoculture could soon result. There is also the question of 'weeds', principally common farmland weeds like docks, thistles and nettles, but also plants common in damp areas like the poisonous water hemlock. In the paradise of open virgin soil, such plants can grow and spread incredibly rapidly and take over the whole area, soon making it impossible to establish anything 'nicer'. My preference is for a light touch, where dense random groups of plants are introduced, but plenty of space is left between groups to allow for some 'weeds' to grow for a naturalistic effect. The dense planting within groups helps to prevent other less desirable species from muscling their way in.

Around a large pond with a perimeter measured in hundreds of metres, manual maintenance and weeding is not realistic. It's important not to stretch out whatever is available or affordable at a fixed distance apart all around the margins, or a very boring appearance may result, so if your budget is under pressure, don't be tempted to plant thinly; instead use densely planted patches and large gaps if necessary. Larger marginal plants should be spaced at 3 to 5 per square metre and smaller varieties at 5 to 9 per square metre. If plugs are used, consider doubling these numbers to allow for some failures. More on planting later, and please remember the advice in Chapter 1 regarding fish and wildfowl.

CASE STUDY: 200M² POND BUILT USING A GCL

Step 1: Mark out perimeter and no-go areas. Establish survey posts as a reference.

Step 2: Strip off turf from tip site and whole pond area and stack away from dig area.

Step 3: Strip off remaining topsoil and stack separately.

Step 4: Excavate the bulk of the subsoil and transfer to tip site.

Step 3: The site has been excavated to level, the topsoil stacked nearby and all the subsoil taken to a tip site.

Step 9a: Detail of unrolling the GCL.

Step 4: The bulk of the pond excavation is complete.

Step 8: Beginning to unroll the GCL.

Step 9b: Sealing the overlaps with granular bentonite clay.

Step 5: Excavate the last metre or so of subsoil to the edge profile required. Ensure that marginal shelves are wide and flat and at the correct depth.

Step 6: Manually pick over the area for large stones or projecting roots.

Step 7: Lay a necklace of land drains connecting to a point lower than the deepest part of the pond, if deemed necessary.

Step 8: Unroll the underlay, if applicable, and then the liner at right angles to this.

Step 10b: Trimming off the excess.

Step 10a: Trenching the ends of the liner.

Step 10c: Backfilling and tracking in the perimeter trench.

Step 11: Returning topsoil to the pond and banks.

Step 9: Overlap edges and joins by 30cm. Pour granular bentonite clay between the seams as an added seal.

Step 10: Dig a trench above water level to hold the ends of the liner. This must be above maximum water level and usually must be on the closest level area rather than on the sloping bank. Terminate the ends in the trench and cut off the excess to just below ground level. Backfill and track in the trench to make a tidy result.

Step 11: Cover the GCL with at least 30cm of top-soil. Use the turf pile for the bottom of the pond, reserving the cleaner topsoil for the shelves and edges. Lightly compact the topsoil layer.

Step 12: Check depths of shelves; most should be 1–10cm below water level. There is usually a little settlement to allow for.

Step 13: The construction is finished.

Step 16a: The pond three months later.

Step 14: Setting out for planting.

Step 16b: The pond one year later.

Step 13: Landscape and tidy up the area around the site, profiling the tipped subsoil and covering with the remaining topsoil.

Step 14: Landscape marker spray is very useful when marking out the planting plan on the ground.

Step 15: Allow to fill and settle, planting bottom dwelling plants such as water lilies when there is just enough water to cover them and marginals just before the water reaches its maximum level. Regular weeding at this stage will pay dividends in the future.

Step 16: Enjoy the result. Water plants grow remarkably quickly, and after a year it will look as though the pond has been there for ages.

Step 15: Planting has been completed.

CHAPTER 5

PLANT SELECTION

Once you have finished building and filling your pond you will have the exciting job of buying all the plants you need. Obviously, you will have researched and planned this at great length and will know exactly what and how many to buy, and certainly won't be rushing out to the nearest aquatic centre and buying anything you fancy willy-nilly! Unfortunately, many do follow the latter path, and will have ample time to reflect on how much better it would have been to take the former. So many people end up with a pond full of invasive and ineradicable thugs due to lack of fore-thought and sheer enthusiasm. Fortunately, since you are reading this book, you are several steps ahead.

It's very common for those with limited knowledge of aquatic plants to assume that there is a limitless range of possibilities regarding selection, but actually the range is very much smaller than that of the panoply of garden plants in general and there is little need to be worried about choosing. In reality there are few that fit any one narrow requirement. It's a much better plan to first consider which plants will fulfil certain functions in the pond, and only once these groups have been out-lined, select the most appropriate for your pond size and look. Fancy colour schemes should take a low

priority until then and may never be realistically achievable.

It may be helpful to first consider the different zones that you wish to plant, based on the depth of water found there. Commonly you will see diagrams of the pond and its surrounds segmented into four or five planting zones. Firstly there is the deepest zone in the pond, where depth exceeds 40cm or so; this zone may be suitable for oxygenators, floating and deep-water plants (*see* Chapter 7) and water lilies (*see* Chapter 8). Next is the deep marginal zone, between 10cm and 40cm of water, where some of the larger and taller marginal plants can be grown, together with some of the smaller deep-water plants. Then comes the shallow marginal zone, from 10cm below water level to about 10cm above, where those plants too short to cope with deeper water will thrive. Marginal plants are described in Chapter 6. Lastly, from 10cm above water level to dry ground is the zone where moisture-loving plants find the right conditions. If you calculate the area that you wish to cover in each of these zones, it will help you to draw up your list. In practice, most ponds will have only two or three zones, housing all the types of plants.

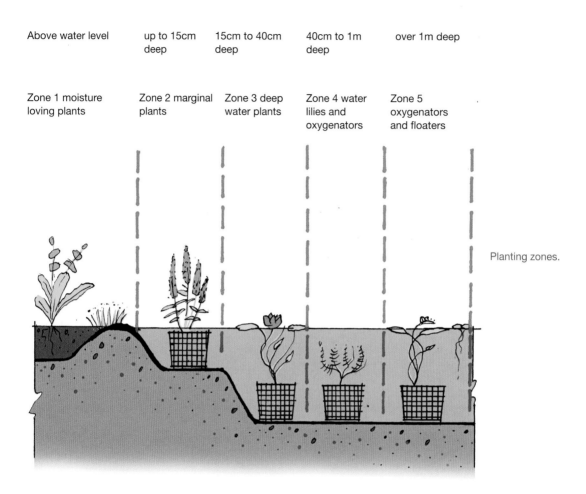

Above water level	up to 15cm deep	15cm to 40cm deep	40cm to 1m deep	over 1m deep
Zone 1 moisture loving plants	Zone 2 marginal plants	Zone 3 deep water plants	Zone 4 water lilies and oxygenators	Zone 5 oxygenators and floaters

Planting zones.

NATIVE PLANTS

Many will wish to use native plants, or predominantly native plants. This is an excellent principle and will ensure that your pond offers the best possible habitat for native invertebrates and larger animals, since many have evolved in tandem with these plants for millennia. If your pond is large and closely connected to the wider environment, you should consider the exclusive use of native plants to avoid any risk of non-native ones starting to colonise the wider environment. There are many examples of native insects which rely solely on certain native plants for their reproduction, and there may be many more yet to be discovered. Generally though, invertebrates seem to be just as happy in ponds containing a mixture of native and non-native plants. Amusingly, one of the plants that newts prefer in which

to fold up their eggs is the now-banned *Lagarosiphon major* (*see* Chapter 9), an invasive pond weed from foreign shores. The soft reflexed leaves provide just what they are looking for. Before taking too rigid a stand therefore, it is wise to consider the wider implications, especially for smaller ponds. Firstly, you must understand that small, isolated ponds on the scale of the average garden pond scarcely occur in nature. Natural ponds are short-lived and on a geological time scale soon silt up, progressing through bog and heath to woodland. Semi-permanent natural ponds either form from sections of rivers that have become separated from the main channel, or in geological depressions or flooded valleys. The plants which have evolved to grow in such locations are typically fast-growing opportunists and many are unsuitable to plant in a garden pond, since they would overrun it in a very short time. Therefore, the choices of native plants suitable for a small garden pond are relatively few.

Some take things even further and only introduce native plants found in their locality. This is an admirable principle, and would be beneficial to wildlife, but I fear might result in a rather limited visual appeal; if that's not an issue for you then it would have the highest environmental value. It can be hard though to find out just which species these might be.

However, provided that care is taken not to introduce plants which would become a problem in the wider environment, the look and diversity of a garden pond can be greatly improved by using some carefully selected non-native plants. Many will be readily consumed or utilised by our native fauna in just the same way as native plants. For example, nearly all our native aquatic plants flower early in the season, which means that nectar is in very short supply later in the summer when many insects are building up supplies to carry them through the winter. A few good clumps of *Pontederia* (pickerel weed) will provide a steady source of big flowers full of nectar from August to October, and the bees and hoverflies won't care that they are from distant shores. They are also non-invasive and

Pontederia isn't native but it extends the season for wildlife.

clumping in habit, which makes them easy to control if necessary. Similarly, there is only one native *Nymphaea* species, *N. alba*, and this is a large and rumbustious plant which would soon take over your small pond. It produces a lot of thick green leaves but relatively few flowers and is not a particularly suitable resident for your modest garden pond. There are however hundreds of beautiful *Nymphaea* cultivars (many of which include a considerable chunk of *N. alba* DNA) producing a lot more flowers, and therefore nectar, which would be much less trouble. They seem to attract just as many, if not more, visiting insects and so a pragmatic gardener might come to the conclusion that there is absolutely no harm in choosing a lily more appropriate to their pond size in preference to the only native one available.

GENERAL REQUIREMENTS AND HABITS OF AQUATIC PLANTS

Regarding the general requirements of aquatic plants, they require exactly the same considerations as any other kind of plant. They need light, nutrients and yes, water! In more specific terms, aquatic plants, including marginal and deep-water plants, need to grow in soil that is completely saturated with water, and sometimes completely submerged in water within a specific depth range. They have no need of root hairs to absorb water since it is in plentiful supply. This contrasts with moisture-loving or damp-loving plants, which cannot tolerate waterlogged soil but simply require elevated levels of moisture during the growing season. Such plants need well aerated conditions not found in waterlogged ground and their root hairs will die off in such areas.

SURVIVAL STRATEGIES

Plants in general have evolved to follow various strategies for survival and reproduction, and these affect their suitability for any given situation. There are three main groups based on these strategies:

- **C strategists** are very competitive plants which steadily form dense cover and bully out their competitors. Examples would be *Carex riparia* and *Phragmites australis*. Only a lack of nutrients would restrict their growth and dominance.

- **R strategists** (ruderals) are plants which colonise new areas rapidly by seeding prolifically, such as *Lychnis flos-cuculi* and *Mimulus guttatus*. However, after a few years they are outcompeted by taller and more competitive species, and they slowly disappear.
- **S strategists** are stress tolerating plants which have evolved to grow in conditions that other plants can't tolerate, such as very acid or nutrient-poor soils. Examples are orchids and carnivorous plants like *Sarracenia*.

Of course, most plants exhibit characteristics typical of more than one of these traits and this will establish their preferred niche.

Maintaining the look

A planted pond often looks its best two or three years after planting, because all the original plants will still be present in more or less the same ratio as that in which they were planted, but as time goes on the C strategists will out-compete the R strategists, and by year five some thinning and replanting may be required to maintain the desired look. If no action is taken, the result will eventually be a monoculture of the most vigorous and invasive varieties.

Some plants are extremely invasive and will form a monoculture, like *Phragmites communis*, Norfolk reed.

PLANTING MEDIUM

Regarding the medium in which to plant them, one needs to remember that aquatic plants mostly evolved to grow in rich water-borne sediment and therefore grow best in soil high in nutrients. However, such soil is apt to create water conditions high in nutrients too, which encourages the growth of unwanted plants such as algae. Therein lies the paradox: you need high nutrient levels for the best plant performance, but low nutrients in the water to discourage excessive algal growth. The compromise is to pot the plants into fine meshed aquatic baskets, with or without an additional hessian or cloth liner, containing a compost developed specifically for aquatic plants. The planted pot is then topped off with a centimetre or two of clean gravel to reduce the leaching of nutrients from the surface. New roots soon lock up the soil, though inevitably some is squeezed out of the basket meshes by microbial and invertebrate activity and root growth. An occasional boost can be given in the form of slow-release fertiliser tablets pushed well into the root ball. In natural swimming ponds the bare rooted plants are normally planted into clean sand or gravel; it is usual for the plants to go a bit yellow initially, but after a while they seem to adapt quite well. Detailed planting advice is given in Chapter 9.

Planting compost.

Bog plants

One major source of confusion with terminology is the word 'bog' when used as a prefix, such as 'bog primulas' or 'bog plants'. I don't like the term 'bog garden' for this reason. Most people visualise a bog as an area of totally saturated ground that squelches underfoot and has areas of standing water on the surface. This is not a suitable place to plant many plants thought of as 'bog plants' because it is too wet for them. This goes for most of the so-called 'bog primulas' and many of the big-leaved damp-loving plants such as *Astilbe*, *Ligularia*, *Rodgersia*, *Trollius* and many others. If it is as wet as a proper bog, the only suitable plants are marginal plants. If you want to grow big-leaved, moisture-loving plants like *Rodgersia* next to your pond, the soil level in this area will need to be at least 15cm above the water level in the ground beneath. Creating suitable conditions needs considerable care and detailed advice will be found in Chapter 10.

Eriophorum is a true bog plant, liking acid conditions.

Moisture-loving plants.

Regarding other soil parameters for aquatic plants, most have a broad range of acceptance of pH, water hardness and temperature, though at the extreme ends of the scale they may become chlorotic (yellow sickly leaves) and fail to thrive. If the pH is between 6.5 and 8 most will be fine, but certain groups prefer acid soil, like *Calla* (bog arum), *Eriophorum* (cotton grass) and water irises, while water lilies (*Nymphaea*) prefer an alkaline soil. Water lilies found in shallow sunny lowland ponds will thrive in temperatures up to 50°C, but plants found in shallow mountain streams or cool spring water ponds like *Luronium natans* or *Ranunculus hederaceus* (ivy-leaved crowfoot) will quickly go to seed and disappear at higher temperatures.

If plants are grown in aquatic baskets, regular application of fertiliser, division and re-potting will be required to keep them growing well. Most will need attention at least every second year.

More detailed information on plant requirements will be found in the respective sections describing them below.

BUYING PLANTS

Garden shows like Chelsea and Malvern have a lot to answer for, in that they raise expectations of what plants should look like to unrealistic levels. A show garden designer will start with many thousands of plants and pick the best few hundred to use in the show garden, packed tightly together so that everything is perfect. Some will have been brought on early with heat and others held back with refrigeration, so may be flowering together when they would never do so naturally. This is simply not achievable in the average garden or with an average budget, so you should expect a strongly seasonal display, some weeds, some brown and yellow leaves and naked stems and some weather- and insect-related damage. Plants that have been raised under glass or polythene will look much better than those raised outdoors on the day they are sold, but the latter are the best to purchase, since they won't collapse from shock the next day when exposed to real world conditions. Don't buy too early in the season, as plants will do much better when they are growing strongly and will soon outstrip those planted out earlier. April and May are the best months to get most marginal plants going, or September for water irises or moisture lovers with roots that are slow to establish.

PLANT FORMATS

Plants can be purchased in various sizes and formats; a good place to start is to decide whether you want to achieve a full look straight away (bigger or more plants) or are happy to watch them grow while accepting that there may be occasional casualties on the way. There are of course various advantages and disadvantages of the various formats in which pond plants can be purchased.

Some of the common formats in which plants can be purchased.

Plug plants

Starting from the smallest, plug plants are often available from specialist suppliers, mostly in spring and summer. They come in various sizes including 3.5cm, 5cm and larger diameter and sometimes in deep cells called root trainers. They may be the cheapest option on a per item basis, but it's necessary to price in the lower establishment success. Certain species, such as *Phragmites*, are pretty much guaranteed to succeed if planted at the correct depth at the right time of year and without interference from wild birds; however, the same cannot be said about many other species, especially the more palatable ones. There are many reasons why plugs may not develop into mature plants, including harsh weather conditions, flooding, disease or being pulled up and/or eaten by wildfowl, rabbits, deer, slugs or snails. For very large schemes where competitive tendering is necessary, plugs are often specified, but this is not necessarily the most cost-effective option in the end.

Bare-rooted plants

The next option in terms of price is a bare-rooted plant. These are typically relatively mature plants which will flower the same year if planted in spring. It goes without saying that size and quality can differ widely and that one tends to get what one pays for. Establishment success is more reliable than plugs in most cases, since a bigger plant has bigger reserves, but the success rate is still dependent on planting in the right way and at the right time of year, and birds like Canada geese can wreak havoc if they spot them before they have had a chance to root properly. Once a plant has rooted, birds will tend to just forage among them, pulling off some of the tenderest and greenest leaves, but not killing them. Until then, they are at risk of being eaten or pulled out and dehydrated. Bare root plants are often not that much more expensive than plugs, so are a cost-effective option taking everything into account. Their other major advantage is that since all the soil and weeds have been washed off, there is a very low risk of contamination by either, so they are the de facto choice for those planting natural swimming ponds, or sensitive sites where no risk of introduction of non-native species can be contemplated. Bare-rooted plants are generally available seasonally and mostly in spring and early summer but also in mid-autumn for some varieties. Large numbers may need to be booked well ahead. Bare-rooted plants should not be planted in midwinter. Some plants are extremely fragile and/or fiddly to handle in bare-root form and should always be purchased in a plug or potted format. Examples include *Luronium natans* and *Eleocharis acicularis*.

Potted plants

Further up the price scale come increasing sizes of potted plants, and these are the most widely available option. They start at P7 (a 7cm diameter pot), then P9 (8–9cm across), 1 litre (11cm), 2 litre (15cm) and 3 litre (20cm). Various larger sizes may also be offered. Their main advantage is that they contain a larger and more resilient plant ready to go, but for garden ponds the smaller sizes will still need to be knocked out of their pot to be planted into a larger pot. In this respect it could be argued that they present no special advantage over bare root plants. P9 plants are very often specified for large planting schemes since they are quick and easy to plant, with an established root ball enabling quick establishment, but can stand indefinitely with a little care and maintenance if planting is delayed or carried out over a prolonged period. They can often be the most cost-effective option, taking everything into account.

Price guide

At the time of writing, the approximate prices for each format for commonly available native species are: plugs 80p–£1.50, bare root 90p–£4, P7 £1.50–£4, P9 £2–£5, 1 litre £3–£9. Rare and unusual plants may cost considerably more of course. So, the price is only one aspect that you need to consider, and not necessarily the most important one. Prices for a single plant will typically be about double that of buying by the hundred.

SUPPLIERS

You may have a water plant nursery close enough to where you live that you can go and speak to those who know them the best, in which case I highly recommend that you do, before you have made a single decision. Even if you don't, a phone call or an email would be a good start. However, for those with the knowledge or confidence to know what they want, there are multiple further options.

Sizes of plants can vary widely between suppliers.

For very large projects you may wish to approach a wholesaler or plant sourcing service. If you send them a list, you are assured of competitive prices, but not necessarily the highest quality or range. These businesses often have a relatively high minimum order and may not be really geared up for giving advice, especially when busy in spring. They mostly sell plugs and/or potted plants but don't usually offer many bare-root options and may require considerable notice for these. Be aware that the size of the plant can vary tremendously between suppliers, so take care to compare like with like.

For most people there is the choice between mail order suppliers or retail sites such as garden centres or specialist aquatic suppliers.

Garden centres

Garden centres are mostly supplied by wholesalers within the UK or from the near continent. Many, especially the larger chains, don't have staff that are particularly knowledgeable about these specialist plants, but those that do are worth a visit. Their prices can be competitive but be aware that they may buy most of their stock early in the season, after which it can get progressively cherry-picked and forlorn. The choice of plants tends to be quite uniform and commercial.

Specialist aquatic suppliers

Specialist aquatic suppliers that don't grow their plants on site are still likely to purchase their plants from the same sources, so many of the same comments apply, though the staff are likely to be better informed. They have one distinct advantage in that they will usually stock all the other items that you need to construct most types of ponds, including liners, pumps, filters, and fish, so it could be a one-stop shop.

Mail order suppliers

Mail order suppliers fall into two camps. The first are those who source direct from wholesalers and don't actually carry any stock themselves, let alone grow the plants. When you order from them, they order from the wholesaler and the wholesaler sends the plants direct to you. Sometimes there are three or more people in the chain, and the person you are dealing with could well be a fifteen-year-old in his back bedroom, since he is just a middleman with a computer, and needs to know nothing about the plants. You won't get any advice or after-sales service worth having and the prices won't be particularly competitive. Many of the bigger companies operate in this way.

The other sort of mail order supplier is the small specialist nursery that grows all or most of their plants on site. Their staff know all about the plants, because growing and looking after them is what they do every day. Their range will be considerably greater than that found at general plant retailers, quality is likely to be high, and their prices will usually be competitive. They

Specialist stalls may be found at garden fairs.

will typically dispatch the plants the same week to arrive at your door in perfect condition, often at a cost less than that of travelling to their door. A visit is highly recommended though, and even if they are an hour or two away you will probably be well rewarded.

Other sources

Lastly there are purchases from garden fairs, village plant sales and gifts from friends. Beware the latter two especially. The reason that people have plants to spare is quite likely that they have taken over their own pond and are now surplus to requirements, in which case you probably don't want to repeat the mistake in your own pond. Moreover, they could contain unwanted hitch-hikers which could make life a misery for you. My advice would be to spurn all such gifts or at the very least to quarantine them for a considerable period before planting them in your pond. Garden fairs are a good hunting ground, as they attract specialist suppliers from out of the area which you may be unaware of.

SEASONALITY

As with all varieties of plants, none look good all of the time, but all will have seasons of interest punctuated by periods in which they are dormant and/or relatively unattractive. Good plant choice and planting design ensures that when one plant starts to fade, another nearby will take over the job. Quite often you will find

Visit a specialist aquatic nursery for the best selection.

that plants have a few weeks in which they look their best, a few months when they add to the look but do not shine out, and up to six months when they do not contribute. Clearly, in the middle of winter there will be little that looks its best, but even then, a selection of evergreen foliage plants and those with structural form can still add interest.

Evergreen plants

Some varieties of plants help to extend the season of interest right into winter. Evergreen emergent water plants are very few, composed of the *Acorus gramineus* varieties, *Baumea*, some *Carex*, *Iris* and *Juncus*, and *Equisetum*. Remember that even evergreen plants don't look good all the time and usually have an 'off' period, often in early summer, when the foliage is being replaced, though not all at once as in deciduous plants. A few more are technically not evergreen, but winter green to some extent, such as *Zantedeschia* in milder parts of the country. Of the oxygenators, only *Callitriche* species grow actively in winter, and *Aponogeton* and water

Very few hardy water plants are evergreen.

cress continue to grow and flower at quite low temperatures. Plants with tough and/or woody stems and/or interesting seed heads like *Lythrum*, *Thalia* and *Typha* can look good even in decay and when the frost sparkles on them. Some plants give really good autumn colour, such as *Anemopsis* and *Penthorum*.

Some plants offer fantastic autumn colour.

Architectural plants form the backbone of the planting scheme.

Naturally, it's not difficult to find plants that look good in spring and summer. In the UK nearly all plants are looking good later in spring and in summer, and very many flower during May, June and July, but some of the most useful ones are those which start into growth late but continue flowering into the late summer and autumn months. These include many of the big architectural varieties that need extra time to produce big leaves and tall stems, such as *Arundo*, *Canna*, *Cyperus*, *Gunnera*, *Pontederia*, *Thalia* and *Zantedeschia*. There are also a very few varieties, often those from hotter and drier climates, that are summer dormant and do their thing early or late in the year, such as *Aponogeton* and *Zephyranthes*.

IMPORTANCE OF SCALE, TEXTURE AND FORM

Once the issue of seasonality has been taken into account, the next things to consider are scale, texture and form. Remember that flowers may be very beautiful, but are often fleeting, sometimes only lasting a couple of weeks out of the whole year. By contrast, the foliage may be present for nine months or more. For example, all water irises flower during late May and June, with large beautifully coloured blooms which encourage novices to use a lot of these varieties in their planting schemes. The problem is that when they aren't flowering, many water irises look almost exactly the same. There are a couple of variegated varieties, and some foliage is broader or greyish, but the display can take on a rather boring monotone look for much of the year if irises form the majority of the display.

The most important and longest lasting feature for most plants is the foliage, and this is extremely variable. Leaves can be large or small, narrow or broad, rounded, oar shaped, rough or smooth, crumpled or scalloped, stiff or floppy, hairy or shiny, yellow, red, white, blue, grey or purple, stripy, mottled, variegated or many shades of green. They can arise from a rosette on the ground or be held aloft on strong or spiny petioles. In short, the permutations are endless, and this gives an infinite number of possibilities within a relatively small number of available plants.

Many designers worry unduly about colour selection, even when the plants concerned don't flower at the same time. There are of course occasions where, for instance, an all-white display might be required for a pond at a wedding venue (or crematorium for that

Water irises are beautiful in flower, but blooms are fleeting.

Leaf lust.

matter) but colour matching should be low on your list of priorities. I have often been presented with a list of clients' requirements along the lines of 'only blue or purple, no yellow, not over 60cm tall, native and suitable for depth of 30cm' – an almost impossible brief and a far from realistic one. Until someone breeds a native plant with dark green evergreen leaves and scarlet flowers blooming for twelve months of the year, growing in any depth of water, it will be necessary to take a realistic approach to planting design and consider texture and form more closely.

HISTORIC ISSUES

During the last fifty or sixty years there has been a big change in the way that the issue of invasive species has been understood. From the sixteenth century onwards, and especially in Victorian and Edwardian times, it was common for plant hunters to go out, dig up and bring home absolutely anything interesting, with little thought for any possible consequences. Slowly it was realised that once a foreign species escaped into the wider environment there could be many unexpected consequences, and as a result many species have been

Eichhornia crassipes (water hyacinth) used to be a useful plant for summer surface cover, but is now banned.

Azolla (fairy moss) is still a problem in many ponds despite having been banned for years.

Crassula (pygmy swamp weed) is another almost ineradicable pest.

rightly banned from sale. These include such horrors as fairy moss (*Azolla*) and New Zealand swamp stonecrop (*Crassula*), but of course, the genie is still out of the bottle. These two plants are still widespread in the UK and despite import controls and plant passporting, they still crop up in consignments of imported and home-grown plants.

Therefore, one needs to be aware that such problems are possible and act accordingly. Extra care is required when introducing any plants directly into a wild location, even more so if it happens to be a sensitive site such as an SSSI. Regardless of the existence of a phytosanitary certificate, with the best will in the world it is impossible for inspectors to spot the hairlike roots of *Crassula* or the microscopic young stages of *Azolla* in a pallet stacked with forty-five crates of *Carex acutiformis*, so vigilance is necessary in the period after planting to nip any potential infestations in the bud. Purchasing the plants in bare root form can be one way to reduce the risk of unwanted hitch-hikers, but it's not a guarantee that plants are completely clear of weeds.

It's best just to be aware that such problems can occur and act promptly if they become apparent. More recently, several more species have been banned from sale on the grounds that they are invasive if they escape into the wider environment, but since the decision was made by the one-size-fits-all Brussels bureaucrats, there have been some useful plants caught in the net. One such example is water hyacinth (*Eichhornia crassipes*). This fast-multiplying floating plant was previously widely used in the UK for summer surface cover, hoovering up nutrients and reducing problems with algae. It is properly tropical and can't overwinter in the UK, dying back below 10°C and dissolving into mush at the first sign of frost. However, it is a pest in canals and rivers in hotter European countries and hence was banned from sale everywhere. It is true to say though that in the vast majority of cases the decisions have been widely supported by the trade and some invasive plants like *Hydrocotyle ranunculoides* and *Lagarosiphon* are no longer available. Some will, however, continue to create problems all over the country for many years yet.

CHAPTER 6

MARGINAL PLANTS

Marginal plants may be defined as those that have evolved to grow in ground permanently saturated with water and can cope with seasonal drying and flooding to a greater or lesser extent. The limits of their ability to deal with these events depends mainly on their height, rooting system and reproductive strategy. Plants such as *Phragmites* (Norfolk reed) are tall and can cope with permanent submersion of their stems up to about 60cm. Even if they were to be completely submerged for several weeks, and though the top foliage might die off, the extensive system of rhizomes would send up new shoots when the water receded, and dormant seeds would sprout to form new colonies. This applies to many tall and grass-like plants such as *Typha* spp. (reed mace), *Cyperus longus* (galingale) and *Schoenoplectus* (bulrush). Some plants such as *Calla palustris* (bog arum) and *Menyanthes trifoliata* (bog-bean) detach or break off during flooding and float until they can root again somewhere else. Others like *Myosotis palustris* (water forget-me-not) can cope with only a short spell of submersion, but produce masses of seeds that ensure long-term survival.

Big plants grown closely together give a lush result.

Smaller plants with separation give a more restful and architectural look.

If large groups of plants are tightly packed together, the planting will look very lush and bountiful, but if smaller groups are placed with significant gaps between them, a simpler and more architectural result will be achieved.

GENERAL ADVICE REGARDING MARGINAL PLANTS

The single most important thing to remember when planting is to ensure that the plant does not end up too deep in the water. Marginal plants usually have quite a narrow margin of acceptable depth, which is usually stated as 'up to *x* depth' of water. This depth refers to the distance between the surface level of the soil in which the plant is growing and the *maximum* water level. Please note this carefully. If a plant requiring *up to* 10cm of water is planted 10cm below water level in the summer, it could well be that in the spring, after the winter rains, it could find itself in water that is much too deep and fail as a result. The general rule is to plant at the shallowest end of the given preferred depth range. The maximum depth given is just that: a maximum and not a target. Almost unexceptionally, plants will do much better at a very shallow depth, but may colonise deeper areas in time as the plant becomes more mature and develops an extensive root system. If you are unsure about the depth required, a good general rule is the 20 per cent rule, which is that most marginal plants can tolerate depths up to 20 per cent of their mature height. There are exceptions, for example *Lythrum*, which will survive but not thrive as deep as that.

There is a further group of plants such as *Anagallis*, *Lychnis flos-cuculi* (ragged robin) and *Gunnera magellanica*, that are not true marginal plants, since they quickly die if submerged for long or when dried out, but can be treated as marginal plants in the vast majority of garden ponds. They can cope with very wet or saturated growing conditions and so can be grown in mesh baskets within a garden pond as a marginal plant provided that the foliage is not submerged for any length of time. This is because most artificial ponds have a clearly defined maximum water level and are topped up manually in dry weather, therefore plants at the edges are not subjected to long submersion or drying events.

Some short plants can be grown as marginal plants, even though that's not technically what they are.

So, be aware of this and plan your shelf depths accordingly. A plant shelf 40cm deep will be suitable for relatively few residents since the vast majority of marginal plants grow best with the soil level at or only just below water level. A wide, flat shelf 15–20cm below water level is just about right for most lined ponds, since most sizes of marginal plant baskets are between 10cm and 20cm deep. The larger the pond, the larger the clumps of plants are likely to be used, and these will need correspondingly larger baskets and deeper shelves to take them. The largest commercially available aquatic baskets are about 28cm deep, so 30cm could be considered to be the maximum suitable depth for a marginal shelf (*see* Chapter 4).

Important note: the comments here apply to pond shelves where plants are to be placed in baskets. For ponds in which they will be planted directly into soil, the majority of the shelf depth should be 2–10cm (*see* Chapter 4).

GROWTH HABITS

Marginal plants can be artificially subdivided into several groups in respect of their growth habits.

Architectural and structural plants

Architectural and structural plants have a strong silhouette and are often tall and upright. They tend to be late flowering and are used in groups in larger ponds,

Thalia dealbata has a strong architectural form.

Rafting plants help to give surface cover at the margins.

or sparingly as specimen plants in smaller ones. Examples might be *Arundo donax* (giant water reed), *Cyperus* spp. (umbrella grass), *Pontederia* spp. (pickerel weed) and *Thalia dealbata* (alligator flag). One large specimen can be a really good choice for impact, even in smaller ponds.

Rafting plants

Rafting plants such as *Potentilla palustris* (marsh cinquefoil) or *Menyanthes trifoliata* (bogbean) have a horizontal growth habit, forming a branching network of stems and spreading towards the middle of the pond from the edges, forming an excellent hiding place for invertebrates, shading the water and breaking up the artificial edge of the pond. They have persistent stems which means that this network is still present in spring to give cover to spawning amphibians before most of the other plants have started to grow.

Creeping plants

Creeping plants are essentially similar but have soft stems and/or don't spread far from the edges, such as

Creeping plants fill the gaps between larger ones.

Veronica beccabunga (brooklime) and *Ranunculus flammula* (lesser spearwort); planted in patches they help to unify the planting around the margins. They die back in winter however, and don't provide much cover early on. Think of them as fillers between the larger plants.

Stalwarts

Stalwarts are plants like *Caltha palustris* (marsh marigold), *Eriophorum* spp. (cotton grass) and *Lythrum salicaria* (loosestrife), which reliably produce masses of flowers and foliage over a long season, and which normally form a sizeable proportion of the total plant population. Think of them as the flesh on the bones represented by the architectural plants.

Irises provide spectacular blooms, albeit for a short period before fading into the background.

Thugs

Thugs could be thought of as fast-growing and invasive plants such as most *Carex* (sedges), *Glyceria aquatica* (manna grass), *Phalaris arundinacea* (reed canary grass), *Phragmites australis* (Norfolk reed) and *Typha* species (reed mace). They have no place in modest garden ponds but are invaluable in large natural ponds to provide dense cover for wildfowl and other animals, or in the regeneration zones of a filtration system.

Stalwarts like *Caltha* have lots of foliage and can be relied upon for a long season of interest.

Accent plants

Accent plants are those like *Butomus umbellatus* and irises, which have a strong impact over a short period and then fade into the background.

Named varieties

Irises are often purchased as named varieties, and it's important to understand that in most cases they don't come completely true from seed and must be propagated by division to maintain the type. If the seed capsules are not removed before the seeds drop, the clump will become more and more contaminated with plants which are not exactly like their parents. It will then no longer be the variety originally purchased but usually will revert to something closer to the look of the original species from which the cultivar was developed.

LIST OF MARGINAL PLANTS COMMONLY AVAILABLE IN THE UK

Here you will find descriptions of the most commonly available marginal plants with their cultivars, habits, advantages and disadvantages. This isn't an exhaustive list but does include most of the varieties which are likely to be found for sale within the UK. Some specialist suppliers may have available small numbers of plants not in commercial cultivation. New varieties of plants like irises are constantly being developed while others slide into oblivion, so naturally this list may become out of date in time.

Concise information on size, planting depth, flower colour, season, etc., is presented in table form in Appendix III to avoid excessive repetition below.

Acorus calamus (sweet flag)

This plain green foliage plant grows to about 80cm tall and can cope with planting depths of 0–15cm. It was introduced from continental Europe, probably by monks in the sixteenth or seventeenth century, and was often used to strew on floors as the leaves are sweetly scented when crushed. It's very good for natural swimming ponds since it produces little debris and is well behaved in habit, slowly spreading laterally. It's fairly duck proof and easy to grow. There is an attractive variegated cultivar 'Variegatus' or 'Argenteostriatus' which has similar requirements and a similar growth habit. The variegation is clean and well-marked, lasts all season and does not revert. Propagation is by division of the jointed rhizomes. The flowers comprise brown cones among the foliage.

Acorus gramineus (Japanese sweet flag)

Not white with a red spot as the name might suggest (a flag is a plant which grows only in shallow water and hence 'flags' a safe place to cross), but plain green. This is a tough evergreen aquatic grass with narrow leaves to about 50cm high. It seems hard to get in the plain form, perhaps because its ornamental value is limited, but is commonly available in various variegated cultivars. 'Ogon' has leaves striped yellow and green and grows to about 40cm; 'Variegatus' (syn. 'Argenteostriatus') has leaves striped white and green and is a little shorter and less vigorous at 25–30cm. 'Pusillus' is a dwarf plain green form to 10cm high. Other similar and commonly available varieties are 'Golden Edge', 'Hakuro-nishiki' and 'Oborozuki'.

Acorus calamus 'Variegatus'.

Acorus gramineus.

Acorus gramineus 'Ogon'.

Acorus gramineus 'Variegatus'.

Alisma spp. (water plantains)

All are plants which grow readily from seed, with airy candelabra inflorescences of pinkish-white flowers on strong flower stems. The leaves are crispy and succulent and quite easily damaged, being more or less susceptible to *Alisma* smut fungus, which causes unsightly black spots. Their rigid flower stems and open habit make them a favourite landing spot for large insects such as dragonflies.

A. lanceolata *(lance-leaved water plantain)*

The lance-leaved species is the biggest and most vigorous, sending up leaves to a metre and candelabra flowering stems with a multitude of tiny pinkish white flowers to 1.5m. It's easy to grow in water up to 30cm deep and is the least susceptible to *Alisma* smut fungus.

A. parviflorum *(syn.* A. subcordatum, American water plantain)

This species is the shortest, foliage 20cm and flowers to 60cm, with unique succulent spoon-shaped leaves and possibly the densest flower spike, but it is very

Alisma parviflorum.

prone to *Alisma* smut fungus and has a very short season in which it looks good.

A. plantago *(European water plantain)*

This is our native species and midway in size between those above. It can grow up to 30cm deep but does best at 5–15cm deep. It does get *Alisma* smut fungus and can be affected by aphids, but is one of those plants most often selected by dragonflies to ascend for their final moult.

Anagallis tenella.

Alisma plantago.

Anagallis tenella (bog pimpernel)

A dainty creeping native plant, smothered in nectar-rich pink starry flowers which smell strongly of honey in summer. An excellent plant for crevices just above water level and exposed tops of baskets, it will tolerate very wet conditions but is not a true marginal and must not be submerged.

Anemopsis californica (Apache beads, yerba mansa)

This very attractive plant will grow in damp soil or very shallow water and reaches 30cm tall. The leaves, initially a bluish green, turn red and orange in autumn and the unusual cone-shaped white flowers become splashed with red as they age. The foliage and flowers are aromatic. New plants form on runners in late summer in the same way as strawberries.

Apium nodiflorum

See *Helosciadium nodiflorum*.

Arundo donax (giant water reed)

One of the tallest (up to 4m) and most impressive marginal plants, this semi-tropical plant is originally from the Middle East and is now widespread. The strong canes support a grass-like flower in summer

Anemopsis californica.

Arundo donax 'Aurea'.

Arundo donax 'Variegata'.

and the strappy leaves and sturdy stems give a very architectural look. The plain green species is just that, but *A. d. versicolor* (syn. 'Variegata') has the added benefit of cleanly striped green and white leaves. The new shoots are pink, white and green. *A. d.* 'Aurea' is less vigorous and slightly less hardy, to about 2m and has yellow and green striped leaves. Prune off the older canes and feed well when the new shoots emerge to retain a strong variegation. Propagate by laying cut stems in shallow warm water; new shoots and roots will form at the leaf nodes.

Baldellia ranunculoides (lesser water plantain)

This tiny native plant of the *Alisma* family has a strange and unique aromatic smell. It has a rosette of narrow leaves and produces multiple pretty pale pink flowers like those of its bigger cousins. Best in very shallow, sheltered locations and has a fairly short season in which it looks good. Produces new plants on the old flowering stems, also propagates well from seed. Can

Baldellia ranunculoides.

Baumea rubiginosa 'Variegata'.

easily be confused with *Luronium*, but the latter has oval floating leaves.

Baumea rubiginosa 'Variegata'

This is a very useful evergreen rush, producing dense stands of long-lasting foliage to about 1.2m, striped yellow and green. Propagate by division in spring and summer.

Butomus umbellatus (flowering rush)

Surely one of the most elegant native plants of all, *Butomus* is easy to grow and easy to please. It's a rapidly spreading plant and doesn't like being confined in a small basket, so divide, feed and re-pot regularly for best results. The running rhizomes form prolific buds as they grow, and each little bit can rapidly produce a new flowering plant. The native species grows to about 90cm tall and prefers shallow water, rich black mud, and full sun.

Butomus umbellatus.

Butomus alba.

Butomus 'Rosenrot'.

The flowers are exquisite, open, flat and pink, held aloft on fat tubular stems. Dragonflies love these stems to perch on and ascend for their final moult. There are two commonly available cultivars: 'Schneeweisschen' (alba/ albiflorus) has white flowers and 'Rosenrot' has darker pink flowers than the species.

Calla palustris (bog arum)

As its name suggests, this native plant grows naturally in acidic swampy conditions. Creeping stems produce alternate heart-shaped leaves and white flower spathes followed by red berries. The old roots pretty much decay at the end of the season, leaving the plants loose in the soil; winter floods then carry parts of the stem to new places to colonise. Propagate by division or seed.

Caltha leptosepala (broad-leaved marsh marigold)

A relatively uncommon plant from North America, this white flowering marsh marigold has tongue-shaped greyish green leaves to about 20cm and

Calla palustris.

Caltha leptosepala.

unique daisy-like flowers. It behaves much as *Caltha palustris* var. *alba* in that it grows best in damp rather than wet conditions.

Caltha natans (floating leaved marsh marigold)

An unusual and tiny floating or very shallow marginal plant from the far North, increasingly difficult to find and not easy to keep, as it likes very cool and clear water with little competition. The flowers are white with the daisy-like petals arranged around a central green boss.

Caltha palustris (marsh marigold, kingcup)

This common and popular native plant scarcely needs description and can be considered a pond essential. It's one of the first to flower in March, producing masses of cheerful yellow flowers, and if cut back after the flowers are over, will grow another set of foliage and flowers, maybe a third set if this is repeated. It is quite happy in a fair degree of shade, and here will tolerate quite dry conditions, but will also thrive in full sun when grown in water as a marginal. Plants develop as crowns of multiple individuals; leaves are heart shaped, and height is up to 40cm. There have been a number of named cultivars over the years, including 'Auengold', 'Auenwald', 'Marilyn', 'Newlake' hybrids, 'Susan' and 'Yellow Giant' but most are very hard to come by. Propagation is easy from seed or division.

Caltha palustris var. *alba* (white marsh marigold)

A species from Asia, this is a much smaller and daintier plant with white flowers, that needs not quite such wet conditions to thrive. It seems to be fine if the soil is saturated, so long as the crown and foliage are not submerged. The leaves are almost circular and have regularly toothed margins. Mature height is no more than 30cm. 'Himalayan Snow' is a particularly good cultivar, if you can find it.

Caltha palustris 'Plena', or *C. p.* 'Flore Pleno'/'Pleniflorus' (double marsh marigold)

A smaller cultivar to only 15cm high, with pincushion buttons of strong double yellow flowers, this is a great plant for smaller ponds as it is compact and well behaved. Crowns steadily increase as multiple plants; when dividing do not separate to individual plants but leave in small clumps for best results. Like *C. p.* var. *alba*, it likes wet feet but will not do well if the crown is under water.

Caltha palustris.

Caltha palustris var. *alba.*

Caltha palustris 'Plena'.

Caltha palustris var. *palustris*

The giant marsh marigold, previously given the confusing name of *C. polypetala*, which suggests double flowers that it does not have. Albeit not native, this is a great plant for larger ponds where its larger size is in keeping. From the Middle East, everything is bigger and better, including leaves and foliage, and the whole makes an impressive wide clump up to 60cm tall in

Caltha palustris 'Honeydew'.

water up to 15cm deep. New plants develop at the leaf nodes on the flowering shoots. The cultivar 'Honeydew' is widely available, with paler flowers and foliage. Excellent for natural swimming ponds since it contrasts well with the mainly grassy foliage of other commonly used plants.

Canna

There are very many *Canna* species and cultivars; they can often cope with quite wet soil in a border, but there are a number of true water cannas which are suitable for growing in the pond. Be cautious when you find others sold as water cannas; they are more properly described as water-tolerant varieties and won't cope with much, if any, submersion. Proper water cannas include *Canna flaccida*, *Canna glauca*, and the varieties 'Endeavour', 'Erebus' and 'Ra'. They start into growth late but produce large leaves which may be green, striped or purple, and tall robust flower spikes with a succession of yellow, orange or red flowers. They aren't fully hardy and should be overwintered in a drier location protected from frost. Plant in full sun.

Cardamine pratensis (lady's smock, cuckoo flower, milkmaids)

This native plant of water meadows and damp areas sends up masses of pale pink flowers early in the season from a rosette of divided leaves. New plants can be propagated from leaf cuttings. It will cope with totally saturated ground but not any significant submersion of the foliage. There is a very pretty double

Cardamine pratensis.

Cardamine 'Flore Pleno'.

form, 'Flore Pleno' and a few named cultivars such as 'Edith' and 'Diane's Petticoat' for the plant hunters. It is a food plant for the orange tip and green-veined white butterflies.

Cardamine raphanifolia (broad-leaved cuckoo flower)

A much larger relative from across the big pond, with big cress-like leaves, which are edible, and lovely large lilac flowers in spring. Like watercress, this plant likes cool running water in light shade and won't look its best in a warm sunny pond, quickly going to seed in warmer weather. A great plant for a waterfall or stream though.

Cardamine raphanifolia.

Carex spp. (sedges)

This is a massive genus of mostly tough, easy to grow perennial grasses, of which many grow in damp or wet conditions. Quite a lot of these species are invasive and almost impossible to control, so they must be used with care in artificial ponds, but they are invaluable to produce excellent wildlife cover in more extensive areas. There are many more species than those listed below but most of the commonly available aquatic or damp-loving ones are described.

C. acuta *(slender-tufted sedge, acute sedge)*

One of the more rampant native species with running roots, narrow bright green leaves and dark seed heads, to about 80cm tall, growing as a marginal to about 15cm deep but capable of penetrating well up the bank, although it will not survive in permanently dry

Carex acuta.

areas. There is supposedly a variegated form too, though I have never seen it.

C. acutiformis *(lesser pond sedge)*

Another native, invasive and rampant running grower, very similar to the above, producing dense, tough thickets which make great hiding places for all sorts of wildlife. Plant up to 15cm deep, though this plant will struggle out to nearly 60cm deep before giving up. Foliage is slightly coarser and greyer than *C. acuta*.

Carex elata 'Bowles' Golden'.

Carex acutiformis.

C. diandra *(lesser panicled sedge)*

Prolifically seeding species making narrow leaved clumps similar to *C. paniculata* and growing to 15–20cm deep.

C. elata *(tufted sedge)*

A clumping species from which the variety 'Aurea' or 'Bowles' Golden' is derived. The golden-leaved form is particularly attractive, with butter-yellow young foliage developing a narrow green margin as it matures. Black seed heads contrast well with the pale foliage and the plant prefers a little shade in which it shines out. The plain species has pale green leaves. Both are suitable for damp or wet ground but don't grow to any great depth.

C. grayi *(Gray's sedge)*

This is a well-behaved clump-forming species growing to about 60cm, that rarely seems to set seed under UK conditions but is a worthwhile addition to the

Carex grayi.

somewhat shadier edges of the pond. Plant in damp soil above water level, where the strange Sputnik-shaped seed heads can be enjoyed. Dark green foliage stays green for much of the year.

C. muskingumensis *(palm sedge)*

Another slower growing, rather delicate species that looks quite like a miniature bamboo. It's very attractive but the stems are easily bent over by wind or wildlife, so it's best suited to a protected planting situation in shallow water. The leaves form an umbrella at about 60cm high. There are various cultivars of which 'Little Midge' is one to look out for, very suitable for smaller oriental themed ponds.

Carex panicea.

Carex muskingumensis.

C. panicea *(carnation grass)*

A shorter and rather less vigorous native species with blue-green leaves and black seed heads, most useful in smaller ponds.

C. paniculata *(greater tussock sedge)*

An uncommon UK native sedge slowly forming huge clumps in marshy ground to 2m or more tall, with fine airy seed heads and narrow drooping leaves. The dense crowns provide cover for many small mammals and insects.

C. pendula *(weeping sedge)*

A very common native sedge of wild places, this can be a nuisance weed in a perennial border or gravel path, but is absolutely appropriate for a waterside setting. The strappy evergreen leaves and drooping seed spikes are good habitat, and this plant will tolerate quite dry soil if it is in a shady position. You won't have to worry about propagation as it will happily propagate itself! Prefers a position close to water level.

Carex paniculata.

Carex pendula.

C. pseudocyperus *(cyperus sedge, hop sedge)*

This native sedge has light green leaves and spiky hop-like seed heads. It's in the middle of the range as far as vigour goes, can be short lived but can easily be propagated from seed, suitable for up to 15cm depth. Height 60–70cm.

Carex pseudocyperus.

C. riparia *(greater pond sedge)*

Possibly the strongest and most invasive native species, this one will grow in depths up to 60cm once established but should be planted no more than 15cm deep. The leaves are coarse and stiff, greyish green and quite sharp edged and the black seed heads stand out well. The whole plant stands 90–120cm tall. There is also a very nice, variegated cultivar *C. r. variegata*, which is much shorter and very much less vigorous at about 50cm, with very clean green and white striped leaves which start off almost completely white in

Carex riparia.

Carex riparia 'Variegata'.

spring. *Carex riparia* 'Bowles' Golden' is a beautiful clump-forming grass with arching golden-yellow leaves edged in green, hard to find now and often actually *C. elata* 'Aurea', also referred to as 'Bowles' Golden'. Years ago I believe that the former was Bowles' Golden sedge and the latter Bowles' Golden grass, but I am now unable to back this up.

Chrysosplenium oppositifolium (golden saxifrage)

This widespread low-growing and creeping native saxifrage is rarely seen for sale but is an excellent ground cover, growing on damp soil or in shallow water, preferring a cool and slightly shady position. The pale green and yellow leaves and bracts form an attractive carpet over the edges of waterfalls and small streams. *C. alternifolium* is similar, with alternate leaves instead of opposite ones.

Cotula coronopifolia (golden buttons)

An obliging, prolific but short-lived plant of shallow water, making large rafts of pale green foliage with a profusion of yellow button flowers. It grows fast in cooler conditions, rapidly going to seed in hot weather

Cotula coronopifolia.

but getting going again when things cool down. Easy to grow and especially useful at the edges of smaller ponds for surface cover.

Cyperus alternifolius (umbrella grass)

Not completely hardy, but suitable for southern parts of the UK, is this lovely architectural papyrus-like grass. It has multiple dark green leaves on sturdy stems to about 120cm, the leaves radiating from the leaf stalk like an umbrella. It can be planted up to 20cm deep to protect the crown from frost but prefers a very shallow situation. New plants can be propagated by floating bent-over or severed heads in water. Sometimes sold as *C. involucratus*. *C.* 'Haspan' is a semi-dwarf variety to about 80cm, more common on the near continent, with a similar look but less showy umbrellas. There is also *C. alternifolius* 'Gracilis' and 'Nanus' and allegedly a variegated cultivar, though I have been unable to source this.

Cyperus alternifolius.

Cyperus longus (sweet galingale)

A rapidly spreading and tough native plant with a similar look to the above, much used in natural filtration systems where it is planted as a monoculture in a segregated planting zone. It prefers shallow water but will spread down to about 20cm in time. Propagation is unlikely to be an issue, but be aware of the sharp new shoots which have the potential to penetrate pond liner – place baskets on a slate or additional layer of woven landscape fabric as a precaution.

Cyperus longus.

Cyperus papyrus (true papyrus)

A very elegant umbrella grass with the look of an exploding firework. Sadly, this plant is tropical and won't survive a UK winter outdoors. However, it can be overwintered indoors as a houseplant and placed in the pond for the summer. There is a dwarf form, *C. p. percamenthus* and 'Nana', too.

Cyperus papyrus.

Cyperus rotundus.

Cyperus rotundus (nut sedge)

A rampant weed in some American states, this is a short sedge producing attractive dark spherical seed heads. Plant with caution.

Dichromena

See *Rhynchospora*.

Dulichium arundinaceum (dwarf water bamboo)

A versatile pretty plant for sun or shade, this one doesn't like being split or transplanted too often and is prone to its stems being broken down, but is undeniably attractive with its spiralling leaves. 'Tigress' is the variegated form and is highly ornamental with a stripy look. Flowers are brown grassy tassels, but the foliage is the star.

Eleocharis acicularis (needle spike-rush)

This short grass-like plant can grow like an underwater lawn in clear water or can grow above water level in

Eleocharis acicularis.

saturated soil. Underwater, it is more or less evergreen, but frost or strong sun will brown off leaves exposed above the surface.

Eleocharis palustris (common spike-rush, painter's brush)

A tough and rapidly spreading native plant which is one of the few shorter groundcover plants to compete successfully with taller invasive plants. Useful for native planting schemes.

Eleocharis palustris.

Equisetum spp. (Dutch rush)

A group of properly prehistoric plants which evolved before the appearance of leaves and flowering plants. The green canes are banded in black and have longitudinal silicaceous ridges, topped by a spore-bearing tip. This led to their widespread use as pot scourers, often sourced from Holland, hence the common name.

E. fluviatile *(river horsetail)*

Once the staple species offered, this is now hard to find, and has largely been superseded by *E. hyemale*.

E. hyemale

Invasive and widespread European plant of marshes and damp ground, steadily spreading and throwing up clumps of hollow canes to 1.8m tall. It prefers to be planted above water level. There is an even more statuesque form 'Robustum' whose canes can be up to 25mm diameter.

Equisetum hyemale.

E. japonicum

This 'species' is in fact a group of closely related plants from Asia, whose canes are often a slightly darker green. Otherwise, similar to the above.

E. scirpoides

This dwarf species to about 15cm tall is, if anything, more invasive, difficult to eradicate and not recommended unless closely confined.

Eriophorum spp. (cotton grasses)

Widespread denizens of marshy ground, these are true bog plants, liking acid swampy conditions. All produce tufts of cottony flowers, waving above the grass-like foliage; the native species are 50–60cm tall and prefer shallow acid conditions.

E. angustifolium *(narrow-leaved cotton grass)*

The most widespread native species, forming large colonies on many moors and upland areas. This plant prefers cooler conditions and may flower poorly in warm areas. The foliage has attractive red and bronze tints.

Eriophorum latifolium.

Eriophorum angustifolium.

E. latifolium *(broad-leaved cotton grass)*

This clumping native species is much less common and has rather shorter and slightly broader and paler green leaves, supporting a very tall stiff flower spike with multiple, often three, pendent cotton wool flowers. Very elegant and less aggressively spreading than the narrow leaved species, it sends out runners to form new clumps.

E. russellianum *(bronze cotton grass)*

A much shorter species with fine hair-like leaves that are almost round in section and beautiful russet-coloured flowers. Significantly less vigorous than the

Eriophorum russellianum.

other species and can be rather shy to flower. Not a UK native and sometimes sold under the incorrect name of *E. russeolum*.

E. vaginatum *(hare's tail cotton grass)*

A native species with fine hair-like leaves and single flowers, initially held vertical but drooping as the flowers open. Slightly shorter than the other native species at about 30cm.

Eriophorum vaginatum.

Filipendula spp. (meadowsweet)

A variable genus of plants from wet and marshy conditions worldwide, these can only barely be described as marginal plants, though they will grow in absolutely saturated soil.

F. palmata *(Siberian meadowsweet)*

Species from the sub-Arctic with dissected leaves and plumes of white flowers. 'Kahome' is a particularly attractive cultivar with pleated and dissected bright green leaves and magenta-pink fluffy flowers, about 60cm tall.

F. rubra *(Queen of the prairie)*

Usually sold as the cultivar 'Venusta', this tall plant grows to about 2m and is topped by big plumes of pink flowers; an impressive back-of-border plant. Although this meadowsweet will tolerate saturated soil it prefers a position above water level.

Filipendula rubra 'Venusta'.

F. ulmaria *(meadowsweet)*

Our well-known native species, liking wet marshy ground in which the low stems can creep and spread. It produces a white fluffy plume of scented flowers from mid to late summer. There is a sterile double form, 'Plena', with pretty, spherical flowers.

Filipendula ulmaria.

Geum rivale (water avens)

Often thought of (and sold) as a marginal plant, probably as a result of the common name, but actually more comfortable in waterside areas where moisture

Geum rivale.

levels are high and may sulk when used as a marginal plant unless the basket is placed so as to stand above water level. This plant produces nodding bell flowers of maroon and brown over a very long season, and if regularly trimmed back will flower from April to September. Height about 30cm.

Glyceria maxima (manna grass)

A very invasive native grass species often found in rich soil along the banks or in shallow reaches of rivers, the long lax stems easily topple and root again, spreading rapidly as a result. Best used as a large bed where cover for wildfowl is required and not suitable for anything other than large areas.

Glyceria aquatica.

G. maxima *variegata (variegated manna grass)*

Scarcely less vigorous but undeniably attractive, with new stems appearing in pink, white and green stripes. Can be used in pots with care, but keep it away from less vigorous plants as it will quickly overrun them.

Glyceria aquatica variegata.

Gratiola officinalis (water hyssop)

This native plant produces multiple soft stems covered with small narrow leaves bearing white starry flowers in profusion. Its lax nature means that it is best planted close to something stiffer like *Lythrum* to give it support, or it can be rather untidy, forming loose mats. Grow in water to about 15cm deep.

Gunnera manicata (Brazilian rhubarb)

Producing the largest leaves of any herbaceous plant, this well-known and barely hardy species starts growing in April and produces huge leaves to 2m or more across on long, sturdy and prickly stems. The flower is flame shaped and produces massive amounts of seed, few of which will germinate under UK weather conditions. There is currently a considerable amount of debate over identification of the two most commonly seen large species. *G tinctoria* (Chilean rhubarb) was banned from sale in 2018 on the basis that it was beginning to spread very quickly in sensitive locations such as the Western Isles of Scotland, since it germinates more readily from seed. Since then, it has become apparent that identification is not as simple as previously thought and a recent research paper published by RHS Wisley contends that **all** *Gunnera* sold in the UK and most of Europe for over 100 years have been hybrids proposed as *G. cryptica*. Reference: Julian M. H. Shaw, Dawn Edwards, John David, Royal Horticultural Society, Wisley, Woking, Surrey, U.K. *British & Irish*

Gratiola officinalis.

Gunnera manicata.

Botany 4(3): 364–384, 2022. Pictures in many older books are wrongly captioned, adding to the confusion. Giant *Gunnera* leaves can be flattened or funnel shaped, and varying amounts of red colouration can be present in the leaf veins, buds and flowers. It has to be said that. in the UK at least, both giant species and/or hybrids are widely planted in parks, gardens and stately homes causing no problems at all and in most locations an environmental disaster is highly unlikely, but pending further changes in legislation, buy from a reputable supplier and never plant out in the wild. Several other large *Gunnera* species exist but are not in cultivation.

There are also several much smaller *Gunnera* species, of which two are worth mentioning.

G. magellanica

A creeping plant with circular pleated dark green leaves, growing to only 10cm high. It has miniature flower candles which tend to be hidden under the foliage. It makes a very attractive understorey to taller plants with naked stems, like *Lythrum*, and prefers a wet soil just above water level.

Gunnera magellanica.

G. perpensa

A medium-sized species, growing to about 60cm high, with coarse heart-shaped leaves and striking hooked purple flowers. It is quite invasive, spreading from seed as well as steadily marching along, but makes excellent ground cover in moist to wet soil.

Gunnera perpensa.

Helosciadium nodiflorum (fool's cress)

Previously *Apium nodiflorum*, this is a very common native plant of streams and ponds, making large loose mats of stems and foliage and apt to mob out smaller, more delicate plants. It is actually edible, with a carroty smell and flavour, but doesn't really compare in culinary terms with true watercress (*Nasturtium aquaticum*). It grows in still or moderately fast running water to about 30cm deep.

Houttuynia cordata (orange peel plant)

So called because of the aromatic leaves and foliage, this is a very rampant plant in damp borders, where it can be virtually ineradicable. It does have a place in aquatic baskets, where it can be confined (to a point) and in filtration systems, where the rapid growth is a bonus. The flowers can be single or double white pompoms and the foliage is dark green with variably coloured markings. Several cultivars exist, with varying amounts of red and purple colours in the foliage, including 'Boo-Boo' and 'Flame', the latter having strong orange colouration. The variegated form has single white flowers, and the cultivar 'Chameleon'

Houttuynia cordata 'Chameleon'.

has beautiful leaves with cream, red and green patches, being rather less vigorous than the species. Autumn colours of all varieties feature dark red and purple.

Hydrocotyle spp. (pennyworts)

H. ranunculoides is now banned from sale due to its invasive tendencies, but these plants give fast surface cover. The rounded and toothed leaves are very attractive and make good cover over pot edges and waterfall margins. *H.* 'Nova Zealand' has small, plain, dark green scalloped leaves and *H. sibthorpioides variegata* ('Crystal Confetti') has frilled leaves edged in pink and white. Beware others which might be rather rampant.

Hydrocotyle sibthorpioides 'Variegata'.

Iris spp.

These are a group of plants which are extremely well known, yet widely planted in the wrong locations, since although they all look similar, the different species have completely different growing requirements. At the risk of over-simplifying, there are broadly three groups. The first are the true water irises or flags, which grow as marginal plants in shallow water or in soil that is completely saturated all the time. The most commonly available examples are *Iris laevigata, I. louisiana, I. pseudacorus, I. versicolor* and *I. virginica*. Then there are the damp-loving irises, typified by *Iris ensata, I. setosa* and *I. sibirica*; these like a higher than usual moisture level in the soil and will cope with occasional inundation, but will rot if kept permanently immersed. Annoyingly, one sees these regularly sold in aquatic baskets as if they were suitable for planting in water. Many hybrids between these two groups are available and they are intermediate in their habits. Lastly there are the border irises such as *I. japonica* and *I. pallida*, which like baking hot and very dry conditions and will soon rot to mush if planted in wet soil.

I. laevigata *(rabbit ear iris, Japanese water iris)*

A lovely plant from the Far East, it thrives in shallow water at the edges of lakes and rivers, preferring a low pH soil. It can be difficult to grow well under typical UK conditions and takes a long time to make a good clump, but has gorgeous big blue flowers and broad light green foliage. It seems to be susceptible to root rot and is best moved or divided only after flowering. Many choice cultivars have been developed, including: 'Snowdrift', which has six-petalled white flowers with a central light purple streak on each petal; 'Royal Cartwheel', with a six-petalled dark blue/purple flower; 'Dorothy Robinson', similar but with lighter blue petals; 'Colchesterii', with white falls heavily marked with purple and narrow leaves; and 'Mottled Beauty', which has a variably marked white flower spotted and blotched in blue, probably a seedling of 'Colchesterii'. *Iris laevigata* 'Variegata' is the well-known variegated blue Japanese water iris, shorter and sturdier at about 60cm but with the same dark blue to purple flowers. The broad, cleanly striped foliage lasts all year and does not fade, so looks good long after flowering has finished. Unusually, this variegated cultivar seems

Iris laevigata.

Iris laevigata 'Dorothy Robinson'.

Iris laevigata 'Colchesterensis'.

Iris laevigata 'Snowdrift'.

Iris laevigata 'Mottled Beauty'.

Iris laevigata 'Variegata'.

Iris louisiana 'Ann Chowning'.

Iris louisiana 'Black Gamecock'.

Iris louisiana 'Heather Stream'.

stronger than the plain species if conditions are less than perfect. There are numerous others, but I have personally tried many and failed dismally to get them to thrive. Perhaps in different soil chemistry they might do better, but most aquatic suppliers have given up with them. While the vast majority of flowers on all varieties will be produced in late May and June, some produce sporadic flowers throughout the rest of the season too.

I. Louisiana

The Louisiana group is not technically a species but a group of closely related species which readily inter-breed to make hybrid plants. The fact that some of these hybrids produce viable seed proves their close relationship. Most of the varieties sold as *Iris louisiana* are cultivated hybrids rather than species, but it is still possible to obtain true species such as *I. fulva*. There are hundreds of named varieties now sold, in every conceivable combination of colours, and their popularity waxes and wanes. Under UK growing conditions

Iris louisiana 'Her Highness'.

Iris louisiana 'Sea Wisp'.

Iris louisiana 'Spicy Cajun'.

I. pseudacorus *(yellow flag)*

This well-known native plant needs little introduction. ('Flags' are plants which grow in shallow water and as a result 'flag' a safe place to cross a river or marsh.) Yellow flag is a particularly vigorous water iris, growing

they can be very shy to flower (our summers just aren't long or hot enough) and some varieties hardly ever do, so although their blooms are huge and beautiful, they have limited possibilities in the UK. They are however easy to grow and make big plants very quickly, remaining almost evergreen in milder areas. In this respect they are valuable, producing foliage which lasts almost all year round. Possibly their biggest drawback is that due to their fast growth, they leave behind a lot of older yellowing leaves and can look rather scruffy at times as a result. For best results, trim, divide and replant frequently in well fertilised soil.

Iris pseudacorus.

Iris pseudacorus alba.

Iris pseudacorus 'Berlin Tiger'.

Iris pseudacorus 'Bastardii'.

to 1.5m tall and making robust clumps in water up to 30cm deep, though not much more. It will cope with prolonged dry periods and will grow pretty much eve-rywhere except very dry soil. It's a bit too much of a thug for small ponds unless regularly thinned but is excellent in larger ones as a 'backbone' of planting, having the bonus of broad strappy dark green leaves and reasonably prolific lemon-yellow flowers. If yours isn't flowering well it probably needs to be divided and fertilised, and this needs to be done quite often. It's a very good plant for natural swimming ponds or water

Iris pseudacorus 'Crème de la Crème'.

Iris pseudacorus 'Flore Pleno'.

Iris pseudacorus 'Holden's Child'.

Iris pseudacorus 'Holden Clough'.

Iris pseudacorus 'Krill'.

Iris pseudacorus variegatus.

Iris pseudacorus 'Roy Davidson'.

filtration systems due to its hungry nature and fast growth. All the *Iris pseudacorus* varieties will grow well and still flower in moderate shade. Again, many selected varieties are available, and these can be a better choice for most garden ponds. 'Alba' is a strong cultivar with alabaster coloured flowers. 'Bastardii' is unfortunately named, but a nice strong plant with a slightly grey/blue look to the foliage and smaller pale cream flowers. 'Crème de la Crème' seems hard to find now, but is the whitest of all. 'Flore Pleno' has fully double flowers but can be short-lived and is nothing like as strong as the species. A number of named cultivars have various amounts of maroon/brown netting on the yellow petal background and are thought to be the result of crossing with *I. foetidissima* or *I. versicolor*. 'Holden Clough' is an old selection which is semi-evergreen, prefers damp rather than wet conditions, and has smaller flowers. 'Berlin Tiger' is similar with rather more strongly marked stripes. 'Holden's Child' is unique, preferring the true water iris conditions and sporting a lovely purple flower with the typical striped and netted yellow throat marking. It's not as tall as the species but is a good strong and sturdy plant. *Iris pseudacorus variegatus* is the variegated sport, having leaves with well-marked cream and green variegation until later in the summer, when the variegation becomes less apparent. It's easy to grow in wet or damp conditions and really shines out in shady spots. You may also find 'Roy Davidson', 'Roy's Lines', 'Roy's Repeater', 'Krill' and others.

I. pseudata

Iris pseudata are hybrids between *Iris pseudacorus* and *Iris ensata* and various named cultivars exist, though they are not popular and are hard to come by in the UK.

I. versicolor *(blue flag, American water iris)*

This species from the northern USA is one of the best choices for marginal planting. It's strong, but not invasive, reliably produces multiple mostly blue or purple flowers per plant and has handsome strappy mid-green leaves which last all season. It can be planted up to 15cm deep but will do better in very shallow water. As one might expect with a plant which has been in

Iris versicolor.

Iris versicolor 'Rowden Cadenza'.

Iris versicolor 'Kermesina'.

Iris versicolor 'Rowden Concerto'.

cultivation for a long time, there are quite a number of named selections, however many are very similar to each other. Seed grown plants will exhibit quite a range of colours and forms from grey through pink and blue to purple, but many are not stable and their offspring will be different. Some of the best were produced and named by Galen Carter at Rowden Gardens in Devon and are sold with the Rowden prefix and a range of music-themed names such as 'Rowden Cadenza', 'Rowden Concerto', 'Rowden Nocturne' and so on; they are still fairly widely available. The cultivar 'Kermesina' has magenta flowers and slightly broader leaves and is deservedly very popular, slightly shorter

Iris versicolor x 'Regal Surprise'.

Iris versicolor x *robusta* 'Gerald Darby'.

Iris versicolor x *robusta* 'Dark Aura'.

too, though watch out for commercially produced seed raised plants which don't conform well to type. 'Regal Surprise' is a tall sterile hybrid with *I. pseuda-corus* to 1m, with purple flowers marked with veined yellow and white. Two very similar cultivars, hybrids with *I. robusta*, are 'Dark Aura' and 'Gerald Darby'. Both have almost completely purple new leaves and strong purple colouration at the base of the mature leaves and purple flowers. There are many other fairly common varieties. There is no variegated cultivar of *Iris versicolor*.

I. virginica

This species comes from the USA and there are various cultivars, the best-known being 'Pink Perfection' and 'Orchid Purple'. This species is robust and pretty much evergreen, with broad and rather floppy leaves to about 80cm tall, and these evergreen leaves can help

Iris virginica 'Orchid Purple'.

Iris virginica 'Pink Perfection'.

with winter interest. Flowers are not particularly prolific though.

Isolepsis cernua

Previously grouped with *Scirpus*, *Isolepsis cernua* is the so-called fibre-optic grass, with small white flowers at the tips of the grassy foliage. It will grow as a marginal, where the look can be best appreciated, or completely submerged where it acts as an oxygenator. Cut back hard after flowers fade to get fresh foliage and more flowers.

Isolepsis cernua.

Juncus spp.

A genus of tough rushes with foliage remaining green for a large part of the year and leaves which are mostly circular in cross-section with a pithy core, but not technically evergreen. There are many species and cultivars, but only those in the following pages are likely to be found in the UK.

J. effusus

J. effusus is the common native soft rush found everywhere in damp fields, marshes and pond edges, with brown flowers clustered near the tip of the leaves. It's a

Juncus effusus.

real thug, seeding everywhere, hard to dig out and can easily mob out weaker plants. Its place is in larger wild settings only. 'Spiralis' is the commonly seen corkscrew form, though a corkscrew variant can also be found for other *Juncus* species. 'Gold Strike' is variegated green and yellow but prone to revert.

J. ensifolius

J. ensifolius is an odd man out, with flattened, sword-like, almost evergreen leaves, and is also native. The cultivar 'Flying Hedgehogs' is commonly available, and you don't need me to tell you what it looks like!

Juncus inflexus.

Juncus ensifolius.

J. inflexus

J. inflexus is the native hard rush, with stiffer leaves and a rather blue/grey look to its foliage. It's attractive, but still invasive and must be used with care in confined settings. 'Afro' is the corkscrew form of this species.

Other commonly available species include *J. xiphoides*, *J. submodulosa*, and *J. acutiflorus*.

Justicia americana (water willow)

It's hard to understand why this isn't more widely available, since it is a short and compact plant which has twiggy stems supporting narrow light green leaves and exquisite orchid-like flowers of purple and white. It's easy to grow and can be simply propagated by tearing apart.

Justicia americana.

Lathyrus palustris (marsh pea)

The sweet pea genus has this single native semi-aquatic species, with a lax scrambling habit of thin wiry stems and small pink flowers. It's a good plant for the wet edges just above water level, but is a background plant rather than a star performer.

Lobelia chinensis.

Lathyrus palustris.

Lobelia spp.

Most lobelias are plants of well-drained, alpine, or even dry locations, but there are a few which can cope with a wetter spot. There are numerous named hybrid culti-vars, but none of these are true water plants. The only properly aquatic one is *Lobelia chinensis*; the remainder listed here are often sold as marginal plants, which they are not, preferring damp feet and dry foliage. They are, to a man, martyrs to slugs too.

L. chinensis

A very pretty and dainty aquatic for shallow water, this looks like a miniature spreading version of the hanging basket lobelias, growing rapidly in late summer, pro-ducing many new plants on runners. The flowers are white.

L. fulgens

A firecracker of a plant, with purple leaves and scarlet flowers in late summer, but only if you can keep the snails and slugs off. The variety 'Queen Victoria' is the most commonly available, but you'll be doing well if it reappears the next year.

Lobelia fulgens.

L. siphilitica, *syn.* L. gerardii

Has pale green leaves and light blue flowers and a rather lax habit, but is more reliably perennial than

Lobelia siphilitica 'Alba'.

Lobelia vedrariensis.

Lobelia 'Hadspen Purple'.

the others, often appearing voluntarily from seed. 'Alba' is the white-flowered form. This species is the least bothered by molluscs. 'Hadspen Purple' is worth mentioning, a hybrid cultivar with royal purple flowers.

L. vedrariensis

Looks very similar but with purple flowers. They are best thought of as annuals to brighten up the late summer display, with any that overwinter being thought of as a bonus.

Luronium natans (floating water plantain)

Previously *Alisma natans*, it displays many of the features of *Alisma*, though is much smaller and daintier. It will grow in shallow water, where the oval leaves float on the surface and dainty white flowers are held just above the surface, or as a marginal where it looks quite similar to *Baldellia ranunculoides*.

Luronium natans.

Lychnis flos-cuculi (ragged robin)

The well-known native plant of water meadows and other seasonally or permanently damp places. It's a ruderal plant which colonises bare ground rapidly but

Lychnis flos-cuculi 'White Robin'.

Lychnis flos-cuculi.

Lychnis flos-cuculi 'Jenny'.

eventually gets displaced by larger and bulkier plants. The dissected pink flowers are held well above the rosette of slightly tatty leaves and flowers are produced over a long period. It produces masses of seeds from which new plants can almost form a turf on bare ground. It can tolerate a position in a mesh pond basket provided that the leaves are not submerged, but prefers to be planted just above water level. The white form (alba) occurs naturally, but there is an improved cultivar called 'White Robin' which has better flowers, rivalling the native pink-flowered species. There are also dwarf cultivars such as 'Nana' and 'Terry's Pink' and double-flowered ones such as 'Jenny' – all are very pretty.

Lycopus europaeus (gypsywort)

A native plant which has rather nettle-like leaves dotted in black and small white flowers, it's rather too invasive for small areas so is best reserved for larger wildlife schemes. It gets its name from the curious folklore that gypsies used the juice to darken their skin.

Lysichiton camtschatcensis (white skunk cabbage)

Has an unattractive name deriving from the rather foxy smell of the leaves and flowers, which can admittedly be quite strong when there is a big patch in full flower, but it is a spectacular specimen plant for boggy ground or shallow water, producing huge paper-white spathes in early spring followed by very large pale green oval leaves in a rosette. Like many plants with thick white roots, it grows slowly, and dislikes being disturbed, so it's best to buy a good-sized plant at the start and grow in a very large and deep pot, or – better still – deep rich black mud. The yellow variety seen in almost every country estate garden (*L. americanus*) has been banned from sale due to its tendency to spread downstream; the seeds are much more likely to germinate and produce new plants than those of *L. camtschatcensis*, which rarely produces many seeds and has never produced volunteer plants in my garden. Hybrids of the two are possible (*L. hortensis*), giving a strong plant with creamy coloured flowers.

Lycopus europaeus.

Lysichiton camtschatcensis.

Lysimachia spp.

This large genus of mostly yellow-flowered plants contains several species of use in a water garden.

L. nummularia *(creeping Jenny)*

A very versatile creeping plant, capable of growing from a drier position outside the pond and into the

Lysimachia nummularia.

Lysimachia nummularia 'Aurea'.

water, forming a raft, or even vice versa. It's one of the best plants for camouflaging poorly executed edge areas or the top of plastic planting baskets, where it won't interfere with taller specimen plants. The native species has bright green leaves and yellow flowers which are borne in profusion; the golden variety 'Aurea' has bright golden-yellow leaves too but of course the flowers don't show up so well on this one. Many garden cultivars exist too, with striped or mottled flowers.

L. punctata *(golden candles, dotted/spotted loosestrife)*

A very adaptable plant with running roots, growing in soil from wet to dry and shade to sun. Its favourite position would be damp soil in part shade, where it produces masses of lemon-yellow flowers in the leaf axils and can quickly overrun other plants, but it's not a proper marginal plant. 'Alexander' is a well-marked variegated variety, with pink and white new leaves maturing to green and white later.

Lysimachia punctata.

L. vulgaris *(yellow loosestrife)*

A similar but native species for similar planting positions. It's happy to grow in very wet conditions as long as the stems aren't submerged.

Lysimachia vulgaris.

L. thyrsiflora

L. thyrsiflora (not *L. thrysiflora* as often given) is tufted loosestrife, which produces pompoms of yellow flowers on willow-like erect stems and is happier in wet conditions than the aforementioned species. It is also native to the UK.

There are numerous other *Lysimachia* species which are suitable for the areas above water level and can link the pond planting to the wider environment.

Lythrum salicaria (purple loosestrife)

Purple loosestrife differs from the yellow loosestrifes in having a persistent square section woody stem and shrubby habit, though new shoots do not form on the old wood the following season but arise from the base of the woody stems. In the USA this is considered an aggressive neophyte, but here where it is native it seems not to cause problems. It does readily seed about and is one of the few plants that can be used as an accent among such thugs as *Typha latifolia* without becoming overrun. The mauve to rose purple flowers come quite late, in July and August, and are produced in profusion, being very popular with all kinds of insects. Apart from losing the lower leaves later in the season and producing masses of seeds, this plant produces little debris and is a popular choice for natural

Lythrum salicaria.

Lythrum salicaria 'Blush'.

Lythrum salicaria 'Robert'.

swimming pools. Many excellent cultivars exist: 'Blush' produces pale pink flowers and is rather a leggy plant; 'Robert' is more compact with flowers that are bright pink; 'Robin' is very similar. There is also a similar species, *L. virgatum*, of which there are two varieties commonly sold as pond plants: 'Dropmore Purple' and 'Rosy Gem'. These don't do that well in a marginal basket but prefer simply moist soil.

Mazus reptans (Chinese marshflower)

This attractive creeping plant has small bright green pleated leaves and blue flowers, reminiscent of garden *Campanula*. It can flower very early in mild weather but browns off easily in frost. The white-flowered variety *M. reptans* 'Alba' is equally attractive.

Mentha spp.

The mint family contains several species which are very useful water plants. Their rambling, creeping and

Lythrum virgatum 'Dropmore Purple'.

Mazus reptans.

Mazus reptans 'Alba'.

Mentha aquatica.

rafting habit provides masses of habitat opportunities, their flowers provide nectar, and their aromatic smell is released when crushed underfoot.

M. aquatica

The common or garden native water mint seen almost everywhere, with dark green leaves with purple accents and similarly coloured creeping stems. It is undoubtedly a bit of a thug, like most mints, but is a valuable plant for wildlife, producing large rafts in shallow water.

M. cervina (Preslia cervina, *water spearmint)*

The mintiest mint, with a powerful spearmint aroma when crushed. It's really good used on a pebble beach where access to the pond is made, where the amazing perfume is released when the plant is trodden on. Not native, this one.

Mentha cervina.

M. pulegium *(pennyroyal)*

Looks rather similar to *M. aquatica*, but the mature leaves are slightly downy with a spearmint smell, and the older stems twiggier and more upright. It's another native plant with multiple homeopathic uses from a flea/mite/mosquito repellent to various less savoury uses such as an abortifacient. The concentrated oil is quite toxic, and tea made from the leaves should only be used in small quantities.

Menyanthes trifoliata.

Mentha pulegium.

Menyanthes trifoliata (bogbean)

A fantastic native wildlife plant with an unassuming common name. The green jointed floating stems send up three-lobed leaves and bear exquisite white flowers in spring, spreading from the banks into shallow water and creating large rafts which act as cover for a myriad of creatures. The long roots trail below the stems, taking nutrients directly from the water as well as from the underlying silt. An essential for any wildlife pond.

Mimulus spp. (monkey flower)

Often thought of as native because of their wide distribution, this genus is not native but widely naturalised. Some are wildly invasive, producing huge amounts of seed in explosive capsules, spreading rapidly into any damp areas, whereas some such as *M. ringens* rarely produce new plants naturally from seed. There are many brightly coloured garden hybrids.

M. guttatus

The spotted monkey flower, available in a wide range of cultivars with red to yellow flowers, often marked and blotched with contrasting shades in the throat.

Mimulus guttatus.

M. luteus

The yellow monkey flower, with plain yellow flowers with no or tiny throat markings.

Both of these species are seriously invasive and should be used with care.

M. ringens

The lavender monkey flower, from the Northern USA, is much less vigorous; it is slender with delicately coloured flowers.

Mimulus ringens.

Monochoria hastata

(Previously *Pontederia dilatata*.) A tall proper marginal plant with dark green oar-shaped leaves. It is very similar to *P. lanceolata* but has paler blue flowers which can sometimes be reluctant to open in cooler summers. The leaves are slightly broader and generally more stripy too. This is a great specimen plant, quickly forming large stands.

Myosotis palustris (water forget-me-not)

Surely one of the best-known plants, growing rapidly, seeding everywhere and producing hundreds of small pale blue flowers among slightly downy creeping stems and leaves. It's not the same as the terrestrial species that comes up in gardens (*M. sylvestris*), which will quickly go black if planted in water. All

Monochoria hastata.

Myosotis palustris.

Myosotis palustris 'Alba'.

forget-me-nots go leggy very quickly, so in order to maintain an attractive look throughout the season, it's necessary to cut back and grow new plants from cuttings frequently; it couldn't be easier. There are a few cultivars of the aquatic species worth mentioning: 'Alba' or 'Snowflake' has white flowers and is daintier and less vigorous; 'Mermaid' is an improved cultivar with purplish stems and bigger leaves and blue flowers; 'Pinkie' has pink flowers and 'Maytime' is a variety with cleanly variegated white and green leaves. The latter is extremely difficult to keep going and is one of those 'Marmite' plants – you'll either love it or hate it!

Myosotis palustris 'Maytime'.

Myosotis palustris 'Mermaid'.

Myosotis palustris 'Pinkie'.

Nasturtium aquaticum (Rorippa)

Our native edible watercress, preferring cool moving water but also growing in the edges of still water until it goes to seed as the temperature rises. Easily propagated from stems bought from the supermarket!

Oenanthe fistulosa (tubular water dropwort)

A vigorous native plant with finely divided leaves reminiscent of those of carrots, and attractive flat umbels of white flowers. It's a bit of a thug and has lax stems which can flop over and smother smaller adjacent plants but is excellent in larger wildlife ponds.

Nasturtium aquaticum.

Oenanthe fistulosa.

Oenanthe javanica (water parsley)

An Asian species, most commonly encountered as the cultivar 'Flamingo' from Korea which has variegated pink, white and green shoots and leaves. The flowers are relatively insignificant, so it's best to cut the plant back hard and frequently to encourage fresh, well-coloured growth.

Oenanthe javanica 'Flamingo'.

Orontium aquaticum (golden club)

A unique plant with blue-green leaves that bead up water as droplets and curious white pencil-like flower spikes with yellow tips. Like Lysichiton, this species has thick white roots which are slow to recover from damage, so it's best planted in a large and deep pot and left undisturbed. It's often sold as a 'deep-water' plant, which is misleading – the leaves will float if planted up to 50cm deep, but it will have a lot more impact if planted just below water level.

Orontium aquaticum.

Peltandra virginica.

Peltandra virginica (green arrow arum)

Comes from the eastern US and has broad green floppy leaves, some of which are arrow shaped, and curious narrow tubular white to green flowers followed by green berries.

Penthorum sedoides.

Penthorum sedoides (ditch stonecrop)

An unusual perennial plant which produces new shoots from unpromising black remnants of the previous year's stems. The stems bear light green leaves with prominent veins and all go bright orange in autumn. Small white flowers do appear in summer too.

Persicaria amphibia (amphibious bistort)

One of the most versatile native aquatic plants for small and large ponds alike, this plant will grow at any

Persicaria amphibia.

depth from wet soil to about 40cm below water level, where the reddish stems grow up to the surface and spread out to make a raft of leaves. Pink bottle brush flowers are held above the water surface in summer. Never invasive and fairly unfussy about its environment, this is a pond essential.

Phalaris arundinacea (reed canary grass)

This aquatic grass is widely distributed, growing as dense stands along the edges of ponds and streams. It's too vigorous for small ponds but makes great cover for wildfowl in larger ponds. The varieties 'Feesey' and 'Picta' have variegated green and white leaves.

Phragmites australis (P. communis, Norfolk reed)

This is the tallest and possibly most invasive native aquatic grass. It's the plant used for thatching and makes dense stands in water up to a metre deep. It's totally unsuitable for small or even medium-sized ponds and should only be planted where its rapid spread and indestructible creeping rhizomes will not cause problems. There is a variegated cultivar with yellow and green striped leaves too, which is hardly less invasive.

Pontederia spp. (pickerel weeds)

A genus of plants from North America which are of great benefit to garden ponds. The lush green foliage is produced late, and only really gets going after the last frosts, but the bulky dark green oar-shaped leaves make an impressive clump and then produce blue bottle-brush flowers over a long period, right into the autumn. These flowers are very popular with pollinating insects.

P. cordata

The basic shorter species, growing to about 60cm high.

P. cordata alba

Has an upright habit and is slightly less vigorous with white flowers.

P. cordata lanceolata

A taller subspecies, otherwise identical to *P. cordata* but growing to 150cm.

Phragmites australis variegatus.

Pontederia cordata.

Pontederia cordata alba.

Pontederia cordata lanceolata.

P. cordata *'Pink Pons'*

Has pink flowers and broader leaves, often growing almost horizontally.

P. dilatata *(royal pickerel weed)*

See *Monochoria hastata.*

Pontederia cordata 'Pink Pons'.

Potentilla palustris (marsh cinquefoil)

This sprawling native plant is very useful in the shallow margins, making a fairly dense raft of red to purple stems which root as they go. The five-lobed leaves are very attractive, being bluish green, pleated and dissected, and the nodding maroon flowers complete the picture. An excellent wildlife plant overall.

Potentilla palustris.

Ranunculus spp.

There are several native species of truly aquatic *Ranunculus*, the larger emergent ones being *R. flammula* (lesser spearwort) and *R. lingua* (greater spearwort). The name comes from the shape of the leaves, so don't worry about them harming your liner since both roots and shoots are soft. There are also species of *Ranunculus* normally thought of as oxygenators, which are described in that section.

R. flammula *(lesser spearwort)*

An excellent native marginal for any kind of pond, albeit quite a promiscuous one; it grows from seed and the flowering stems also produce roots at the nodes. The yellow buttercup flowers are individually small, but very numerous, and give a pleasing effect. It's best in the shallow margins where it scrambles about and fills up gaps between baskets.

R. lingua *(greater spearwort)*

One needs to be a little more cautious with this one in small to medium-sized ponds as it is a bit of a thug; it's simply a bossy bigger brother but has far fewer flowers. The cultivar 'Grandiflora' is widely sold and is supposed to have larger flowers than the parent species.

Ranunculus flammula.

Ranunculus lingua 'Grandiflorus'.

Rhynchospora colorata (previously *Dichromena*) (star grass)

This attractive plant bears airy 'flowers' of white bracts that last for a long time in late summer, it likes a sheltered spot in full sun. Don't cut back in autumn but wait for new foliage to appear in spring before tidying up. It's barely hardy and will not survive any serious frost.

Rumex hydrolapathum (great water dock)

'Why on earth would I want to plant a dock in my pond?' I hear you cry. Because it's the sole food plant of the rare large copper butterfly! It also has huge tongue-shaped leaves and makes a nice contrast from the grassy foliage of many native plants.

Rumex sanguineus (blood dock)

Has leaves with prominent veins of reddish purple, a bit like beetroot leaves, and provided that the old

Rumex hydrolapathum.

Rhynchospora colorata.

Rumex sanguineus.

leaves are regularly trimmed back it will produce plenty of well-marked fresh ones. If you don't want lots of seedlings, cut off the flower spikes before they set seed.

Sagittaria spp. (arrowheads)

The arrowheads are an interesting genus of broadly similar plants with arrow-shaped leaves and white flowers with yellow or black centres. They are true water plants and do best in deep rich mud with a few centimetres of water covering it. You won't be able to buy a big multi-year plant, because these plants grow afresh each year from turions produced at the end of roots the previous season. These turions look like small acorns, are edible and very attractive to wild-fowl, which grub them up and eat them, trashing your planting zone. They have a very short season, the turions sprouting in May and producing leaves in June. The plants grow rapidly and flower in July and August, after which the leaves tend to brown off and disappear quite quickly. There are many species and subspecies and the nomenclature can be confusing; many suppliers refer to various Asian species as *S. japonica*, which isn't a species but a trade shorthand. Most aren't widely available but those below can be found in the UK.

S. australis *(long beak arrowhead)*

Comes, confusingly, from the Eastern US, not Australia, and is sometimes sold as the variety 'Benni Silk Stockings', which has somewhat variegated foliage with prominent netted markings. Flowers are small poached eggs.

S. graminea *(oar-leaved arrowhead)*

A native to the US and Canada, much more prolific than our native species and producing small dirty-white turions and narrow tongue-shaped (not arrow-shaped) leaves and and small white flowers. It's very invasive and best avoided in earth bottomed ponds. The cultivar 'Crushed Ice' has variegated green and white foliage but is much less vigorous, being quite hard to keep going.

Sagittaria graminea.

S. latifolia *(duck potato)*

An American species with large edible pink and white turions, broad pointed arrow-shaped leaves and a yellow centred white flower. Can be invasive in earth ponds.

Sagittaria latifolia.

S. sagittifolia *(arrowhead)*

The European variety, native to the UK. It is unique in having small turions which are greenish (as opposed to white or pink in other species) and produces white flowers with a black centre. It tends to be smaller than the Asian species and is much less invasive. There is a double form 'Flore Pleno', but this is very reluctant to flower and only a small percentage tend to flower in any one season.

Sagittaria sagittifolia var. *leucopetala.*

Sagittaria sagittifolia.

S. sagittifolia *var. leucopetala*

An Asian subspecies; much larger with broad blunt-tipped leaves, yellow-centred white flowers and turions that are pinkish white. This variety can also be invasive. Again, there is a double form, but this is a completely different prospect, with large impressive fully double flowers. The turions can be quite large too, sometimes as big as a walnut.

Sagittaria sagittifolia var. *leucopetala* 'Flore Pleno'.

Saururus cernuus (lizard's tail)

This vigorous running marginal plant has aromatic foliage and roots and makes a lot of growth in one season, though starts late. The upright portion of the stem bears elongated heart-shaped leaves and plentiful hooked fragrant white flowers. The whole plant quickly makes a large raft in the shallows, providing lots of hiding places for invertebrates.

Saururus cernuus.

Saururus chinensis

Rather similar but more upright, less vigorous and bears the occasional variegated leaf.

Schoenoplectus spp. (formerly *Scirpus*)

This is the genus of true bulrushes. Bulrushes are generally perceived as the tall marginal plants with fat brown pokers, but those are in fact reed mace. Bulrushes have thin tubular leaves filled with pith; these were historically used as candles by dipping in wax. The spiky brown flowers are produced near the tip of the leaf.

S. lacustris

Our native grey bulrush or lake bulrush, which is capable of extending deep into the margins and grows up to 3m tall. There are several other species often used in water gardens.

Schoenoplectus lacustris.

S. lacustris tabernaemontani 'Albescens' *(candy striped bulrush)*

Has gorgeous longitudinal stripes of green and white on canes nearly 2m high. It's a great architectural specimen plant but can be easily trampled and broken by wildfowl in bigger ponds.

Schoenoplectus tabernaemontani 'Albescens'.

S. lacustris tabernaemontani 'Zebrinus'

Its non-identical twin, with horizontal green and white banding, not as tall as *S. albescens* at about 1m. Undoubtedly a very attractive plant and a good backbone plant to set off the others.

Schoenoplectus tabernaemontani 'Zebrinus'.

Scirpus cernuus

See *Isolepsis cernua*.

Scrophularia auriculata (figwort)

A common native plant growing in wet places, it's a bit scruffy and lax but produces small sticky maroon flowers that seem very attractive to insects. There is a variegated cultivar too, which tends to be short lived.

Scrophularia auriculata.

Scrophularia auriculata 'Variegata'.

Sparganium erectum (branched bur reed)

Another common native marginal, having long strappy leaves with blunt tips and spiky balls of white flowers, maturing to spiky green seed capsules. It's too vigorous for small ponds but is excellent for larger wildlife ponds. It produces a lot of seeds so spreads quite rapidly.

Sparganium erectum.

Sparganium emersum (unbranched bur reed)

Less common and tends to grow mainly underwater, where the long strappy leaves undulate in the current, but can grow erect as an emergent too.

Stachys palustris (marsh woundwort)

This edible native plant of the mint family isn't truly a marginal but can cope with saturated soil and does come up from below water level, so is included here. The tall bristly stems are quite lax, arising from a network of running white roots, and produce mauve to purple flowers which are popular with insects.

Stachys palustris.

Thalia dealbata (alligator flag)

As mentioned earlier, 'flags' are plants which generally show a safe place to cross water, since they only grow in shallow areas. In this case, *Thalia* is even more useful, because the stiff flower stems topped with purple flowers wave from side to side when an alligator swims through, warning you that he is coming! It's one of the most architectural plants imaginable, with tall oar-shaped leaves which bead up water on their surface. You might also find *T. geniculata* or *T. germinata*, which are quite similar. This plant is known by some as the 'bee assassin' as the flowers trap many insects and some bee species which visit them. If, like me, this bothers you, cut off the flowers and just enjoy the magnificent foliage.

Thalia dealbata.

Typha spp. (reed mace)

Widely referred to as bulrushes, they are not a rush (which mostly have leaves which are rounded in cross-section), but a big reed with flat, strap-like leaves. These spiral slightly, enabling them to stand erect, a remarkable feat if you stop to consider it. Just try to hold upright a 2m-long strip of any thin flat material from one end and you'll appreciate what a wonder it is! All *Typha* produce flowers in the form of a poker at the top of rounded stems which can be up to 3m tall. The pokers vary in size and colour, from the fat almost black ones of *T. latifolia* to the mini dumpy ones of *T. minima*. There are several species used as marginals in the UK, most of which are too large, vigorous and invasive for small ponds. They all have sharp roots which should be borne in mind in ponds with rubber liners.

T. angustifolia *(lesser reed mace)*

This native species is hardly less tall or invasive than its big brother, but has narrower leaves and slightly less sturdy stems to about 2m. The male and female parts of the cigar-shaped mid-brown flower are separated by a small naked gap.

Typha angustifolia.

T. gracilis *(slender reed mace)*

A rather shorter species growing to about 1.5m, with light brown pokers.

Typha latifolia.

Typha gracilis.

T. latifolia *(greater reed mace)*

The largest native species, growing to about 2.4m tall, has broader leaves than *T. angustifolia* and large, fat, dark brown to almost black pokers and will colonise water up to 60cm deep. This plant fixes nitrogen and can increase nutrient levels, affecting water quality.

T. laxmannii *(golden reed mace)*

This has chocolate-coloured pokers of intermediate size.

Typha laxmannii.

T. minima *(miniature reed mace)*

A dwarf species growing to 40cm tall, producing dumpy mini pokers. This species can be shy to flower, needing plenty of fertiliser and a very shallow planting position.

T. shuttleworthii

Sometimes specified for the regeneration zone in natural swimming ponds, this less common variety is slightly less invasive and produces relatively few mid-brown pokers, some of which are slightly egg-shaped.

Veronica beccabunga (brooklime)

A very useful scrambling plant for banksides and shallow water alike, this fast-growing native plant quickly covers bare soil and creates a raft of vegetation in shallow water, either moving or still. The creeping stems root at the nodes and support handsome small dark green oval fleshy leaves and clusters of small blue flowers over a long season.

V. beccabunga is the most commonly offered species, but *V. anagallis-aquatica* can sometimes be found too.

Typha shuttleworthii.

Typha minima.

Veronica beccabunga.

Zantedeschia aethiopica (arum lily)

The waxy white rhizomes are very adaptable, growing in moist soil or just under water equally well. The whole plant is barely frost hardy, so planting just below the water level helps to prevent the tubers from being killed by frost. Even so, once temperatures drop below zero the green leaves will blacken and turn to mush and if the tuber freezes then it's game over. Despite their unsuitability for colder areas, this is a fantastic marginal plant, producing masses of large mid-green leaves and white flowers over a long season. Cultivars include 'Green Goddess', which has mostly green flowers tinged with white, 'Marshmallow', 'White Sail' and 'Kiwi Blush'.

Zantedeschia aethiopica.

Zantedeschia 'Green Goddess'.

Zephyranthes candida (rain flower)

A bulb which produces perfect pure white starry flowers, this is a plant which naturally dries out during hot weather and then flowers en masse when the rains come. When kept permanently wet however it can flower at almost any time, but usually in summer. Other beautifully coloured species are available: *Z. citrina* is a strong yellow and *Z. rosea* is perfect pink, but these species are less keen on permanently wet planting positions.

Zephyranthes candida.

CHAPTER 7

OXYGENATING AND DEEP-WATER PLANTS

Some plants are described as 'deep-water plants' but may not conform to your idea of deep water at all; this is often a source of confusion. One example is *Orontium aquaticum*, almost always described as a deep-water plant. The leaves of this plant will float on the surface if the crown is, say, 15–20cm below the surface, but I hardly think that 15cm should be described as deep. A straw poll of my friends established that most people think of deep water as too deep to stand in, and if so that means that virtually no 'deep-water' plants would thrive here, including *Aponogeton*, *Marsilea*, *Orontium* and many others. Deep water when applied to water plant terminology has somehow acquired the meaning of 'too deep for most marginal plants'.

Oxygenating and deep-water plants occupy pretty much the same niche in the pond, oxygenating plants really being a subsection of deep-water plants. However, the term 'oxygenator' is applied to a specific group of soft-stemmed, fast-growing plants which are much more efficient in transferring oxygen to the water. Some oxygenators can grow to great depth if the water is clear, especially the milfoils. Water clarity is the main limiting factor in how deep they will thrive. By contrast, other 'deep-water' plants in general are less important for oxygen production, since their leaves mostly float and release oxygen direct to the atmosphere, but they

Orontium aquaticum is often termed a deep-water plant, but only does well in shallow water.

Plenty of oxygenators make for fantastic water quality.

Ceratophyllum demersum.

do create much-needed surface cover in the form of their floating leaves.

OXYGENATING PLANTS

These are so called because their daytime process of photosynthesis produces oxygen as a by-product, like all plants. Since the leaves and stems are submerged, this oxygen dissolves into the water as it is expelled from the plant. (Of course, this means that any plant with green material below the surface, whether stems or leaves, can act as an oxygenator.) Because they are fast growing, they can become a problem in themselves, and some non-native species have been banned from sale for this reason. These include *Elodea nuttallii*, *Myriophyllum aquaticum* (*M. proserpinacoides*, parrot's feather), and *Lagarosiphon major* (the latter often incorrectly referred to as *Elodea crispa* or just 'Crispa'). It's also important to realise that like all plants, oxygenators switch to respiration during the hours of darkness – instead of producing oxygen they consume it – so if there is an excess of oxygenating weed in a pond it can lead to de-oxygenation later in the night. This is especially marked during spells of low atmospheric pressure and can lead to fish kills in thundery weather when the water temperature is high, and less oxygen can dissolve in the water anyway.

Some oxygenators grow with their stems and leaves completely submerged, like *Ceratophyllum demersum* (rigid hornwort); some have just the tiny spikes of flowers held above the surface, such as *Myriophyllum spicatum* (spiked milfoil) and *Ranunculus aquatilis* (water crowfoot); some are partially under the water

Hippuris.

Marsilea quadrifolia.

and partially above it, such as *Hippuris vulgaris*. Others, like *Eleocharis acicularis*, can grow either completely submerged like an underwater lawn, or above the surface.

Oxygenators are highly seasonal (*see* Table 7.1 at the end of this chapter) and are normally sold in bunches of several strands clipped together with a small lead strip at the base. They will survive just bobbing around the pond, but most are unlikely to grow well like this, except for *Callitriche* and *Ceratophyllum*. *Callitriche* will grow better if planted or will root into whatever is nearby or just into the water column, but *Ceratophyllum* doesn't grow any roots and it is pointless to try putting it in a pot. The lead strip is mostly just to facilitate portioning and may be insufficiently heavy to sink the bunch to the bottom, so it's much better to pot all the other oxygenators up just like marginals before gently lowering to the depth required. Good garden soil is best to use as a potting medium; firm them well in before submerging and use one bunch per 1-litre pot or several bunches in a 3-litre pot to make a nice fountain of underwater foliage.

DEEP-WATER PLANTS

These are considered to be those that grow mainly submerged, with floating leaves, but can also include those such as *Orontium* (golden club) which can grow with a substantial part of the leaves submerged but some of the foliage held above the surface. This is in contrast to the main body of marginal plants, which mostly grow with all or nearly all of the foliage above the water.

Examples of typical deep-water plants are the coloured water lilies (*Nymphaea*), brandy bottles (*Nuphar*) and water clovers (*Marsilea*). Their primary function for the pond keeper is to produce attractive coloured flowers and/or floating leaves, which shade the water and help to prevent excessive amounts of algae in the water. *Marsilea* is actually a fern, so doesn't produce flowers, but has large numbers of attractive four-leaf-clover leaves. A reminder here about the term 'deep water' – it doesn't mean 6m deep. Most 'deep-water' plants are happiest at depths of 50–90cm and below about 1.5m it is impossible to establish most 'deep-water' plants. Our native brandy bottle (*Nuphar lutea*) is capable of rooting at 3m depth but is then unlikely to produce floating leaves or flowers for many years, until the rhizomes have grown closer to the surface. Until then only soft, lettuce-like leaves will be produced close to the bottom.

Here is a catalogue of the most commonly offered deep-water plants.

DEEP-WATER AND FLOATING PLANTS

Aponogeton spp.

A group of plants from the Southern hemisphere with strongly vanilla-scented flowers and oval floating leaves. There are many tropical species used in aquaria but only two commonly available hardy ones.

A. desertorum *(previously A. kraussianum)*

A species with twin scented flowers and smaller leaves, preferring slightly shallower and warmer conditions than *A. distachyos*.

Aponogeton desertorum.

A. distachyos

One of the most useful plants in depths from 20 to 120cm, especially in cooler or shadier ponds, this prolific plant spreads quickly from seed and produces masses of oval floating leaves to about 20cm long and 8cm wide and profuse white vanilla-scented flowers. Most of the growth and flowers occur in spring and autumn and in sunnier and warmer ponds it may go dormant in hot periods. This is a much better choice than *Nymphaea* in shadier or cool spring-fed ponds since lilies don't flower well at lower temperatures. It's just a pity that it isn't native! Pond snails (*Limnaea*) can really devastate the leaves if they get too numerous.

Hydrocharis morsus-ranae (frogbit)

A sweet little native floating plant with small white flowers and leaves like a miniature water lily. It is

Aponogeton distachyos.

Hydrocharis morsus-ranae.

deservedly popular and a lovely addition to a small pond. It likes hard water and alkaline conditions and prefers a shallow, sheltered spot among other plants with its trailing roots touching the bottom sediment. It has a short season and doesn't like open, deep water in full sun, so in terms of surface cover, it's unfortunately of limited use.

Marsilea species (water clover)

Growing in water up to a metre deep, the water clovers, actually aquatic ferns, produce large numbers of four-lobed floating leaves on rambling stringy stems, steadily making a dense stand. Like *Potamogeton natans* below, its wandering nature means that it won't stay in its pot but will spread widely among the bottom sediment. They are quite late to start into growth but can cover large shallow areas in a short time.

M. mutica *(Nardoo)*

This uncommon Australian species is hardy enough to grow in most lowland UK areas. It has lovely marbled and variegated leaves with concentric markings. In its native Antipodean habitat it is a food plant for Aboriginal people.

Marsilea mutica.

M. quadrifolia *(four-leaved water clover)*

The European species shown earlier, which can be grown as a deep-water plant with floating leaves or a short marginal plant.

Nymphoides peltata (water fringe or fringe lily)

Not a lily at all, despite the floating olive-green coloured lily-like leaves, but related to bogbean. This useful shallow water plant spreads rapidly by means of runners which root at their nodes, producing a profusion of yellow flowers on the surface. It can be very prolific in shallow, earth-bottomed ponds and can shade out submerged plants like oxygenators, being difficult to control in such situations, but can perversely be hard to get going in a typical garden pond with little sediment to get its roots into.

Potamogeton natans.

Nymphoides peltata.

Potamogeton natans (broad-leaved pondweed)

This species is not so much an oxygenator as a deep-water plant but can be found labelled as either. What it lacks in the beauty stakes is at least partly offset by the valuable surface cover it offers. The oval brownish leaves can be confused with those of *Aponogeton*, but its small, brown, knobbly flowers won't win any prizes. It's another example of a plant with rambling runners (like *Marsilea*), which doesn't much like being confined to a pot and won't stay in one for long. In the absence of bottom sediment in a liner pond it is quite likely to

fizzle out after a year or two. In an earth-bottomed pond, it can be very prolific and can spread into areas up to 3m deep, although it does best at depths around a metre. There are very many other species of *Potamogeton* which do much the same job but are rarely offered for sale.

Stratiotes aloides (water soldier)

A tropical-looking floating plant of still water that is in fact native, like the top of a pineapple floating in the

Stratiotes aloides.

pond. Young plantlets are produced on runners, and they can increase exponentially in favourable situations. Ponds with large colonies always seem to have clear water, probably because they absorb nutrients directly from the water and pond bottom via their trailing roots. Plants mostly sink to the bottom in winter, becoming more buoyant as the new growth appears in spring and floating to the surface. Small specimens aren't strongly buoyant and may sink or float on their sides. Short-lived white flowers are produced in late summer. Keep under control in larger ponds; the leaves are rather sharp edged, so gloves are advisable when handling.

Trapa natans (water chestnut)

Another floating plant with a tropical appearance. Hardy as the overwintered nut, it is at the northern limit of its European range in the UK and should be treated as an annual here. The attractive marbled triangular leaves float on the surface, providing useful cover, while the nut acts as a counterweight and anchor. Quite often *T. bicornis* is supplied as *T. natans* but the nut on this species has two horns, the plant looking otherwise very similar.

Trapa natans.

OXYGENATING PLANTS

Callitriche spp. (starwort)

There are very many similar species of *Callitriche* and only a very experienced botanist would stand a chance of identifying many of them correctly, so most are sold

Callitriche stagnalis.

Frogspawn in *Callitriche*.

under the catch-all names of *Callitriche stagnalis* or *C. palustris*. They produce large numbers of soft pale green leaves, the floating ones forming a star-like rosette on the surface, hence the name. Starwort starts growing as temperatures drop in autumn and is the only oxygenator to grow in winter. It's therefore very valuable habitat for early spawning amphibians, especially newts and a multitude of invertebrates. The small soft leaves are just what the newts are looking for in which to wrap up their eggs. It will grow in the bottom sediment or just as a loose mat in shallow water and will inhabit water up to a metre deep.

Ceratophyllum demersum (hornwort)

Possibly the most versatile of all oxygenators, hornwort grows in a loose colony, overwintering as just the short terminal bushy tips and growing rapidly in late spring and summer into large multi-branched loose clumps. It doesn't make any roots at all and so is easily controlled by lifting out any excess. The dense whorled foliage makes excellent cover for tiny creatures. It can be distinguished from milfoils by the horns, or fork at the tip of the leaflets, absent in milfoils. It will grow down to about 3m in clear water (*see* image earlier in chapter). Another species growing in deeper water and looking a little more straggly is *C. submersum*, but although you might find it mixed in, you are unlikely to find it for sale separately.

Eleocharis acicularis (needle spike-rush)

A short, fine aquatic grass that can grow completely under shallow water like a lawn or as a short marginal plant. Underwater it can be more or less evergreen, but above water will brown off in hot sun or frost.

Elodea spp. (curled waterweed)

Generally considered as the black sheep of the oxygenators, species of *Elodea* are extremely good oxygenators but are very invasive, growing in deep water and displacing other species until only a monoculture remains. Several species have been banned from sale for some time, but others are still legally

Eleocharis acicularis.

Elodea canadensis.

available. In my opinion none of them should be used anywhere other than in research.

Note: *Lagarosiphon major*, another banned species, was frequently sold as *Elodea crispa*. This is still widespread in lakes and ponds everywhere and causes a lot of problems.

Fontinalis antipyretica (willow moss)

Scandinavians living in simple stone and turf houses used to use this plant to pack into stone chimneys to make them airtight, since it is quite fireproof. It grows in fast-running water, attached to boulders, or still water if it's cool enough. It is of limited use in most garden pond situations though.

Myriophyllum species (water milfoils)

A large genus, the milfoils are some of the most common of submerged waterweeds and will grow to 3–4m deep in clear water. Several species are commonly available to purchase, some of which are native and some not. Again, there are invasive species which have been banned from sale, but which are still commonly seen, especially parrot's feather (*Myriophyllum aquaticum or M. proserpinacoides*).

M. crispatum *(upright milfoil)*

A non-native species, this has sturdy brittle reddish stems and rigid whorls of bright green leaves.

M. propium

This seems to be a trade name applied to various species of milfoil and is not a recognised species.

M. spicatum *(spiked milfoil)*

Possibly the most common milfoil in the UK, and reputed to appear spontaneously in new ponds, the stems have a reddish hue, and the leaves are dark green, with leaflets arranged like fishbones. It will grow to considerable depths in clear water, possibly as much as

Fontinalis antipyretica.

Myriophyllum crispatum.

Myriophyllum spicatum.

Myriophyllum verticillatum.

5m, but much less in cloudy water. Commonly available from early to late summer.

M. verticillatum *(whorled milfoil)*

Very similar to *M. spicatum* but with longer leaflets in the typical fishbone arrangement, giving excellent habitat for many small creatures. Happiest in water up to 1.5m deep and available as per *M. spicatum*.

Potamogeton spp.

This is one of the most diverse groups of underwater plants of all, from the threadlike network of *P. pectinatus* to broad-leaved robust examples like *P. natans*; notoriously hard to identify given the endlessly variable forms exhibited by even single species. Only a few are commercially available, but you might find unusual varieties such as *P. perfoliatus* offered by specialist local nurseries.

P. crispus *(curled pondweed)*

The bronze-coloured leaves of this plant have wavy margins, making it one of the prettiest oxygenators

Potamogeton crispus.

available, but it has a rather Jekyll and Hyde character. Where it is happy, which tends to be in cool, shallow spring-fed ponds, it can make dense stands and need significant control; however, it can be very hard to establish in warmer garden ponds. It is also hard to transport since it wilts very quickly and turns to mush if it gets too warm. It therefore only tends to be available for a short time in late spring and early summer.

Other *Potamogeton* varieties which you may come across include *P. pectinatus* and *P. perfoliatus*. *P. natans* is sometimes sold as an oxygenator but is listed above under deep-water plants.

Ranunculus spp.

The water crowfoots are the only pondweeds to produce significant numbers of sizeable flowers, which are white in all cases.

R. aquatilis

This has two main forms: the threadlike streamer weed of rivers and the more branched form with threadlike underwater leaves and three-lobed surface leaves found in still water. Preferring fairly shallow and cool water, this is a pondweed which can be hard to establish in small ponds, being easily outcompeted and not liking high summer temperatures. It does produce prolific flowers if it is happy.

R. hederaceus *(ivy-leaved crowfoot)*

A fairly commonly found plant, colonising wet, bare soil such as wet muddy farm gateways. The shiny lobed leaves look good enough to eat but it soon goes to seed and dies back when temperatures rise. It's usually available only in spring for that reason.

Ranunculus aquatilis.

Utricularia spp. (bladderwort)

A group of uncommon underwater carnivorous plants which are nevertheless quite vigorous in conditions which they like, which are clear water of low hardness. The bladders catch zooplankton and the most common, *U. vulgaris*, produces the most exquisite tiny orchid-like yellow flowers.

Vallisneria spiralis (eelgrass)

Can sometimes be found, though it is more commonly sold as an aquarium plant, with long tongue-shaped leaves and sometimes small white flowers, but it is not native and unlikely to thrive in most garden ponds.

Ranunculus hederaceus.

Utricularia vulgaris.

Table 7.1 Typical oxygenator availability

Plant/month	Jan	Feb	Mar	Apr	May	Jun	Jul	Aug	Sep	Oct	Nov	Dec
Callitriche stagnalis												
Ceratophyllum demersum												
Eleocharis acicularis												
Elodea canadensis												
Fontinalis antipyretica												
Hippuris vulgaris												
Hydrocotyle 'Nova Zealand'												
Hydrocotyle sibthorpioides 'Variegata'												
Myriophyllum crispatum												
Myriophyllum spicatum												
Myriophyllum verticillatum												
Potamogeton crispus												
Ranunculus aquatilis												
Ranunculus hederaceus												
Scirpus cernuus												
Key	Usually not available		Sometimes available			Usually available						

CHAPTER 8

WATER LILIES AND NUPHARS

GENERAL CONSIDERATIONS

Water lilies are possibly the most misunderstood plant used in garden ponds. In nature, water lilies grow in fertile mud in shallow warm water and full sun. Most modern cultivars are derived from denizens of much warmer climates than the UK, and most of

Nymphaea alba, the only UK native true water lily.

the commonly available ones were selected and propagated in warm or hot regions of France, USA, Thailand, Australia and China. Therefore, position in the pond is of utmost importance. Your lily can be in sunshine for 24 hours a day, but if the pond is fed from a spring or trickle of water originating underground nearby, the water will be too cold for it to thrive. Underground water in the UK emerges at 10–11°C, whereas lilies require temperatures over 20°C to flower and hardly grow at temperatures below 16°C. Division and replanting should only be carried out at temperatures over 16°C. If you do have a cool pond, *Aponogeton* is a much better choice, since it prefers cooler water and goes dormant at high temperatures.

Many people seem obsessed with depth when constructing ponds, and make the bottom over a metre deep, which means that most water lilies, if placed on the bottom, will struggle. The lilies which you may see in large lakes, growing at greater depth, have most likely been there for a very long time, are not constrained by a planting basket and have access to unlimited nutrients. Given a big enough planting container and enough time, there are varieties which will cope with up to 1.5m of water, but unless you are thinking in terms of decades, the best depth for most lilies is 40–80cm. More on this below, where the various categories of water lilies are detailed.

WHAT'S IN A NAME?

Our only native water lily is *Nymphaea alba*, and this was once distributed around the Northern hemisphere, though localised in favourable spots and absent over large areas. It's important to understand that if you wish to use only native plants, probably for all the right reasons, there are several drawbacks to using *N. alba* in your pond. Namely, given the right conditions it is very vigorous, producing tubers as thick as your arm, masses of plain green leaves and few white flowers, which are often hidden among the leaves. It's far too strong for smaller ponds as it will fill the whole thing in short order. Moreover, there are some historical issues: in the second half of the nineteenth century the Victorian gentlemen were never happier than when they were draining land or digging up some wild plant or other to use for hybridisation. In this way many of the original *N. alba* were dug out and lost. The vast majority of *N. alba* in private ponds and lakes then ended up on the compost heap when all the new exciting, coloured varieties became available, and nobody wanted those rumbustious, cabbagey old things with small white flowers. As a result, the plants labelled *N. alba* today are almost certainly genetically impure and could well be rejects from unsuccessful hybridisation attempts, being discarded back to where they came from. It could well be argued that true *N. alba* has ceased to exist.

There may well be some peculiar insect that relies solely on *N. alba* for its existence, but if there is, I am unaware of it. Any lily will fill the same environmental niche and you are therefore well advised to choose a variety which suits your pond and purpose. If you are really looking for a large variety similar to *N. alba* but with more large white flowers and fewer leaves, 'Gladstoniana' is the closest choice. Much the same applies to the Swedish water lily, *N. alba* var. *rubra*, a red-flowered subspecies. This is now rare in the wild since it was a favourite parent for the likes of Marliac and other European hybridisers, but it is a much better choice than plain *N. alba*.

Hardy or tropical?

The first major division of the true water lilies is that *Nymphaea* may be hardy or tropical. If in doubt, look at the outer edge of the leaf: if it is smooth edged it is a hardy variety; if it is toothed or jagged it is a tropical one. Furthermore, all hardy lilies open their flowers in daytime, whereas tropical lilies may be day or night blooming. Tropical lilies will not be covered in this book aimed at UK readers, since they do not survive UK winters or flower outdoors except in very hot summers. Nor will I cover the other four genera in the Nymphaeaceae family, namely *Victoria* and *Euryale* or *Barclaya* and *Ondinea*. An excellent coverage is offered in a 2005 book by Perry Slocum (*see* Suggested Further Reading for details).

Nymphaea 'Tanzanite', a tropical blue scented lily.

LILY CLASSIFICATION AND GROUPING

Hardy lilies are from two genera, *Nuphar* (the brandy bottles) and *Nymphaea* (water lilies). The *Nuphar* genus contains relatively few members, and the taxonomy is far from clear.

Nuphars

Up until recently, between two and twenty-six species were recognised, including *N. advena* syn. *N. macrophylla* (spatterdock, the American variety), *N. lutea* (brandy bottle, the European one) and *N. japonica* from Asia, together with *N. pumila* (least lily, a smaller variety) and *N. variegata*, but there is now a strong current in favour of classing them all as subspecies of *Nuphar lutea*. All are broadly similar, producing thin, soft, lettuce-like underwater leaves and globe-shaped yellow flowers, sometimes marked with red patches and often held just above the water. If the water is shallow, they also produce thicker leathery olive-green floating leaves of various sizes, the largest being those of *N. japonica*. *N. lutea* can grow at considerable depth, then only producing soft, thin leaves close to the tuber, and is the only cultivar widely available and considered native to the UK.

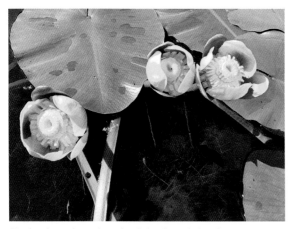

Nuphar japonica rubra, the Asian brandy bottle.

Nuphar lutea, the European brandy bottle.

Water lilies

It is useful to appreciate that there are relatively few true species of hardy water lily. Briefly, these are:

- *N. tetragona* – subspecies are found in the Northern hemisphere, China, Japan and Australia.
- *N. alba*, native to Europe and North Africa with variants in Sweden, Australia and New Zealand. Very many cultivars today have some *N. alba* parentage. Four main variants.
- *N. candida*, native to northern and central Europe and North Asia.
- *N. caroliniana*, from the USA.
- *N. odorata*, native to the Americas from Newfoundland down to Guiana.
- *N. tuberosa*, found in the Northern part of the USA (four variants).
- *N. mexicana*, found in (you've guessed it!) Mexico and the Southern states (two variants).

All the hardy varieties available today have been created by hybridising between these species and their offspring.

The subspecies and varieties of hardy water lilies can be further artificially segregated in many ways. Often, hardy water lilies are split into four artificial categories relating to their vigour and size at maturity. These are: pygmy, small, medium and large. They may also be grouped according to the type of their tubers, though this is now less clear-cut due to the proliferation of hybrid varieties. Tubers may be described as Marliac, Tuberosa, Odorata type, Pineapple or upright, or Mexicana type, in decreasing order of tuber diameter. Slocum also refers to a 'finger or thumb type' for the smallest variants including *N. tetragona*, though this seems not to be universally adopted.

Additionally, they are often described in terms of their flower colour, the five main choices being red, white, pink, yellow or changeable/copper flowers. In water lily parlance, pinks are those with paler pink colours, dark pinks tending to be grouped with the reds. Changeable or copper flowers are found on relatively few varieties, these opening yellow and slowly changing to copper and orange to red, or vice versa. These images are of *N*. 'Comanche' on three successive days.

While there are relatively few true *Nymphaea* species, a huge number of cultivars have been created

Hardy water lily rhizome types.

Nymphaea 'Comanche', day three flower.

Nymphaea 'Comanche', day one flower.

Nymphaea 'Hidden Violet', an inter-subgeneric hybrid lily.

Nymphaea 'Comanche', day two flower.

through hybridisation and cross pollination. This really began with Bory Latour-Marliac in France in the late nineteenth and early twentieth century, and many of his original hybrids are still available today. His nursery was taken over by various families who continued his work and is still in operation today. I thoroughly recommend a visit if you are in the Marmande area. There have been many well-known hybridisers such as the Laydeker family in France, Kirk Strawn and Perry Slocum in the USA, Froebel and Dreer in Europe and the National Botanic Gardens in Australia. Much of the work being done today is in Thailand and China, where there are a huge number of amazing hybrids. There are now many hundreds of different cultivars, with perhaps two or three hundred widely available in the UK, so there is something for everyone.

The elusive blue, scented, hardy lily

Tropical water lilies will not be described in detail in this book since they do not thrive in UK conditions. However, it is important to mention the inter-subgeneric hybrids. These are varieties created by crossing tropical lilies with hardy ones, in the hope of producing blue or purple flowers and/or strongly scented flowers, traits that are absent in hardy lilies but common in tropical ones. (Quite a number of hardy lilies are attributed with scent, but you are unlikely to pick it up unless you are very close.) Every so often a new variety is launched that claims to be a hardy blue and/or scented hybrid, but to date I remain unconvinced by their claims of hardiness, let alone performance, under real UK conditions. It's one thing for the lily to survive, but quite another for it to thrive, so for me the jury is out, especially considering the high cost of such new varieties. So far, any new lilies have had purple rather than blue flowers, in the same way that there isn't really a blue rose; I have no doubt, however, that as our climate becomes warmer and hybridisation attempts continue, there will be the possibility of a hardy blue lily which can be grown successfully in the UK.

LILY SIZE CATEGORIES

Pygmy lilies

Pygmy lilies are very much smaller than the others, with tubers no larger than your little finger and correspondingly small leaves and flowers. They are only suitable for very warm, shallow and sunny positions and will not cope with competition from larger plants or algae. Suitable containers might be a very shallow pond or shallow bowl on a sunny patio or in a conservatory. Another possibility might be a dedicated very shallow zone within or adjacent to a natural swimming pool. There are only three true pygmy lilies: 'Helvola', 'Rubra' and 'Tetragona alba', being yellow, red and white flowered respectively.

Small type lilies

These are a much better choice than pygmy lilies for most small ponds. Suitable for 20–40cm of water depending on variety, they offer a good combination of relatively slow growth with sufficient vigour to produce a good number of flowers. Examples include 'Aurora', 'Burgundy Princess', 'Ellisiana', 'Laydekeri lilacea', 'Snow Princess', 'Solfatare' and 'Walter Pagels'.

Medium type lilies

This group is the biggest and contains most of the varieties suitable for the average garden pond. They have a medium rate of growth and eventual size and are suitable for 40–80cm of water and there is the widest range of choice of flower colour within this group. Many of the changeable varieties are towards the lower end of this category in terms of vigour.

Large type lilies

Sometimes referred to as lake lilies, these are strong, rumbustious plants which are better at coping with less-than-ideal conditions and disturbance from wildfowl, etc. They should be planted at depths of up to a metre, but large established plants can colonise water up to 150cm deep in some cases. Leaves can be up to 50cm across and flowers correspondingly large, so they can be seen at a distance. They are generally too vigorous for smaller ponds.

CHOOSING AND BUYING A LILY

Aside from the depth available for planting, which is probably the most important factor, there are other considerations too. If a large variety is planted in water that is not deep enough for it, the leaves will mound up into a hummock on the surface and hide the flowers. Conversely, if the water is too deep for a smaller variety, the lily tuber will use up its reserves trying to get the leaves to the surface and will produce few leaves and even fewer flowers, eventually running out of energy and failing. At the correct depth and spacing,

A healthy lily will have a lot of leaves.

A healthy lily will have a lot of roots too.

drowned and lost, and the lily will then lose a lot of energy producing a complete new set. If it is already late in the season, this will weaken the lily just before it goes into hibernation and it could fail. In early summer there is enough time for the lily to recover, but the best time to buy is in spring, before the lily has produced any flowers or many mature leaves, and the new leaves can naturally reach the surface before unfolding. Even when the lily has long enough leaf stems to reach the surface, the leaves have an annoying habit of turning upside down when the lily is relocated; if they stay like this for more than a day or two, they will also die, so try to encourage them all to stay the right way up!

A healthy lily in the growing season will have lots of undamaged leaves and plenty of roots emerging from the basket. Don't worry unduly about flowers or buds when selecting one, because lilies flower in flushes and it may not be the right time for it to be producing them. There should not be any plain yellow leaves unless it is late summer, and the lily is starting to die back. In winter there will only be a few small leaves close to the crown, but you shouldn't be buying one then anyway.

Individually, water lily flowers last for about four days, after which they close and sink under the surface, and generally flowers come in flushes rather than being steadily produced, so leaves are important too. To my mind a plain green leaf contrasts well with most flowers. Please note, many lilies whose leaves are green when mature have new leaves that are bronze, red or purple. Some varieties have strongly marked leaves, which can make an attractive show when the plant isn't in flower. Yellow-flowered varieties in particular can have strongly veined, mottled or marbled leaves and they do tend to hold onto their leaves for longer out of season.

Even though some varieties are described as scented, it might be best to disregard this and consider it a bonus, since hardy lilies don't have a strong fragrance and you are unlikely to pick it up unless your nose is right in the flower. If you have space for more than one, I believe that several of the same variety, or at least the same colour, will always look better than one each of several different ones, and the same goes for colours. On my nursery, white lilies outsell all the other colours put together, but white and pink or white and red can look good too. Pink and yellow close by is a hard sell for me, but beauty is in the eye of the beholder, and if you like a riot of different colours then go for it!

the leaves will float flat on the surface and the flowers will be clearly visible. In the UK, water lily growers keep their lilies in shallow ponds or tanks to give them the maximum warmth and sunlight. This means that even large varieties will have short leaf and flower stalks when sold. (Lily leaf and bud stems are very brittle too, so if they are longer, they invariably get broken during transport.) This does mean that if you buy one in full flower and drop it straight to the bottom at a metre depth, all the mature leaves and flowers will be

Leaves of yellow and some pink lilies can have attractive markings.

Step 1: Haul out the overgrown lily ready for division and re-potting.

PLANTING AND PROPAGATING LILIES

Water lilies are easy to grow as long as you follow some basic principles. Lilies can be split and replanted at any time when they are in active growth, which is basically April to August in the UK. After this, the plant is pro-grammed to retreat; its metabolism slows down meaning that new roots will not form, and if cut, the tuber is liable to become infected by fungi or bacteria since it is less able to fight them off.

Most types of lilies grow mainly in one direction until side branches develop, so allow for this by plant-ing the tuber so that the cut end is against one corner or side of the container and the growing tip is aimed towards the opposite side. This allows for the maxi-mum amount of growth before the lily climbs out of the basket at the other side. When breaking up a large overgrown lily, the bits to keep are the terminal lengths of the thickest tubers around the outside. The central part, although it may have small side branches, is best discarded – these bits may grow, but nothing like as well as the outer growth. It's much the same as with perennial terrestrial plants, where the central part becomes woody and unproductive.

Step 2: Cut off most of the leaves and roots.

Re-potting lilies: step-by-step

When you first haul out a lily for re-potting it will prob-ably look like the plant pictured in Step 1. It may be difficult to see where it starts and ends, and it will be

Step 3: Wash with a strong jet of water to expose the rhizomes.

Step 4: Divide the rhizomes into sections with a healthy growing point.

Step 5: Plant the tuber so that soil comes about halfway up the tuber. The best soil to use is a medium to heavy loam.

necessary to clean the whole thing with a strong jet of water. Cut off all the larger leaves and most of the roots until you can see what you are doing. In this case you can see that there were in fact two lilies, one smaller and one larger, and one of the labels is still legible.

To prepare the lilies for planting, trim off all mature leaves and leave just the small ones close to the crown. Make a clean cut through the tuber about 10cm from the growing tip. In the image for Step 5, the sections on the right are scrap and will be discarded.

Trim off all the roots to 2–5cm long, since old roots do not grow again once severed and you must wait for the tuber to produce new roots. These emerge at the junction between the leaf stems and the tuber, so it's best to plant the tuber so that soil comes about half-way up the tuber. The best medium to plant in is good topsoil with a high clay content. If you use a sandy soil, aquatic compost or any other bagged compost, it is quite likely that the lily will float up out of the pot when it is submerged, since the tuber is buoyant, and the sandy mix will not grip it sufficiently. A similar result may occur if you use too small a basket; the leaves, roots and stems all have significant buoyancy and the whole thing can just float to the surface when it starts to grow, especially in a liner pond where the lily cannot root into the bottom.

Half fill the container with topsoil, including one or two slow-release fertiliser tablets if possible and support the lily horizontally, with the tip pointing slightly upwards and the cut end against a corner or side of the basket. Fill around the tuber and keep firming the soil around it and any remaining roots

Step 6: Fill the basket to halfway.

Step 7: Place the rhizome slightly tilted upwards with the newly cut end at the corner or side.

Step 8: Firm soil tightly around the rhizome to leave about half exposed.

Step 9: Top the pot with gravel to prevent the soil from leaching out.

until the container is nearly full, and the tuber is firmly gripped by the soil. Top the pot with a layer of pea gravel to stop soil leaching out of the pot and make a tidy result. Don't bury the tuber completely under the soil or gravel.

Water the potted lily thoroughly before placing it in the pond. This may seem pointless, but what it does is to fill up air pockets with water and prevent trapped air in the soil from burbling out through the compost when the lily is submerged, loosening it up and possibly allowing the lily rhizome to float out.

Finally, lower the lily carefully to cover it and leave in a shallow, warm and sunny spot until new roots are growing through the side of the pot. It can then be lowered to its permanent position. Maximum depths stated on labels are just that, a maximum and not a target, and all lilies will grow best at half their maximum depth. It's very difficult to plant lilies successfully in hessian or cloth bags as it is next to impossible to keep the soil firm when moving and placing them. The best way is to drop a lily that is already established in its basket carefully to the bottom in the correct depth of water. As it grows, the lily will split and burst the basket and will eventually subsume it altogether. If you are trying to establish bare-rooted lilies in a large pond or lake and are tempted to tie them to a brick and drop or lob them in, I don't recommend it – some may survive but you will lose many of them. It's much better to plant bare-rooted lilies in large ponds by draining down until the part normally 90cm deep is exposed, plant them there and then refill the pond. If you can't drain it, or don't have sufficient water available immediately to at least cover the lilies by 15cm after planting, I'm afraid you're just going to have to get wet – cold water swimming is all the rage, I'm told! It's not easy though, and using potted lilies saves a lot of grief.

WATER LILY VARIETIES

Sadly, space does not permit me to describe all the wonderful cultivars available, so here is a selection of those you are most likely to find, and which generally perform well in the UK. If you wish to find out more about these beautiful plants, there are some titles listed in the suggestions at the end of this book. The books by Perry Slocum and Caroline Holmes are particularly recommended. To avoid excessive repetition, I have used only the variety name and have omitted the *Nymphaea* prefix.

Pygmy lilies

Suitable for very shallow, warm and sunny positions only.

'Pygmaea Alba'

Strictly speaking 'Tetragona alba', this is the smallest white lily, with cup-shaped flowers and olive-green leaves. Although not the smallest lily, this variety is not particularly strong or free flowering. 'Snow Princess' or

Pygmaea Alba.

Pygmaea Rubra.

'Walter Pagels' are often a better choice for a small white lily. Planting depth 10–30cm.

'Pygmaea 'Helvola'

The smallest lily of all, this dainty variety has tiny horseshoe-shaped leaves splashed with brown or mahogany markings on a pale green ground. The tiny, pale-yellow flowers are quite prolific and show up well against the leaves. Plant 10–15cm deep.

'Pygmaea Rubra'

The flowers on this variety open pale red and darken gradually over the few days that the flowers are open.

Cultivars of this variety vary widely, and many are probably not true Pygmaea rubra. The leaves are dark green with a purple tinge. Plant 10–20cm deep.

Small type lilies

Suitable for smaller ponds at depths up to 40cm, but preferably 20–30cm.

'Aurora'

This delicate lily has flowers of a variable hue, opening yellow and darkening to a peachy orange and then a pinkish red. The leaves are lightly marbled on a mid-green ground. It's best planted 20–30cm deep.

Pygmaea Helvola.

Aurora.

'Burgundy Princess'

Another good choice for a small pond, the dark red flowers are supported by very dark green leaves. Plant 20–30cm deep.

'Candidissima'

This is a small cultivar developed from *N. candida*, a North American species. The leaves are bright green and show off the white flowers well. The flowers have yellow centres.

'Ellisiana'

A lovely small lily with red flowers contrasting well with mid-green leaves.

Ellisiana.

'Froebelii'

One of my personal favourites, this compact but prolific variety produces flowers that are wine-red and unique dark green shovel-shaped leaves.

Burgundy Princess.

Froebelii.

Candidissima.

'Laydekeri lilacea'

This variety has rose-pink flowers that are slightly scented, set off by mid-green leaves.

Laydekeri lilacea.

'Perry's Baby Red'

One of the best choices for a small pond, this prolific bloomer has dark red flowers and neat green foliage. Developed by Perry Slocum in the USA in 1989.

Perry's Baby Red.

'Snow Princess'

A modern variety, this is a much better choice than 'Pygmaea Alba' in most situations, since it is stronger and flowers more freely. Flowers are paper white and the leaves mid green.

Snow Princess.

'Solfatare'

A variable variety with flowers that open yellow and darken to orange and red, this is suitable for any small pond.

Solfatare.

'Walter Pagels'

A dainty lily with white flowers with just a hint of pink and olive-green leaves, a good alternative to 'Pygmaea Alba'.

'Xiafei'

Bred in China and launched in 2000, this reliable variety has small, fiery red flowers and green leaves edged with a red margin.

Xiafei.

Medium type lilies

Generally suitable for water depths of 40–80cm.

Alba *var.* rubra

This lily found in Sweden is a subspecies of *N. alba* with dark red flowers and plain green leaves when mature. It was used frequently by early hybridisers and is now rare in the wild. It is of medium size and vigour and, coming from northern latitudes, is fairly tough.

'Albatross'

An excellent choice for medium-sized garden ponds, this is a classic lily with plenty of white flowers and plain green leaves, though young leaves are reddish purple.

'Almost Black'

Characterised by flowers of a deep plum colour, this is quite similar to Black Princess but not quite so dark. New foliage is bronze, turning green later. This is not a particularly strong variety and is best in small to medium-sized ponds.

'Albatross'.

Alba var. *rubra*.

'Almost Black'.

'Black Princess'

The darkest flower of all, with very dark red, almost dark purple flowers with slightly incurved rounded petals, making it highly sought after. Not difficult to grow, though the dark flowers can be damaged by strong sun. Leaves are mid to dark green.

'Black Princess'.

'Colorado'

Surely one of the most attractive lilies of all, with cactus-type flowers of salmon pink, held above the water surface. Often flowers quite late and into the autumn and is suitable for medium to large ponds.

'Colorado'.

'Fabiola'

Purported to be identical to Mrs Richmond, this lily has fat tubers and produces plenty of large deep pink flowers and prolific green foliage. A good choice for surface cover.

'Fabiola'.

'Gloire du Temple-sur-Lot'

A fabulous variety for a warm shallow area, fast spreading with smallish green leaves that turn up at the edges to reveal reddish-purple undersides. The flowers are fully double, mid-pink and can be nearly as large as the leaves.

'Gloire du Temple-sur-Lot'.

'Gloriosa'

Green foliage suffused with bronze tints sets off the red flowers very well on this lily of medium size and vigour.

'Gloriosa'.

'Gonnère'

Pure double white flowers are set off well against leaves which are olive green, a good variety for a medium pond.

'Gonnère'.

'Hermine'

A good substitute for *N. alba* in smaller ponds, this useful variety has small olive-green leaves and dainty white flowers.

'Hermine'.

'James Brydon'

One of the earliest and best selections and with teacup-shaped rose-red flowers unique in shape and colour. Leaf stems are red and leaves green with maroon flecks. Reputed to flower even in slightly shaded areas.

'James Brydon'.

'Joey Tomocik'

One of the best yellows, with deep lemon flowers generally held slightly above the water and green leaves flecked, veined and marbled maroon. Good for any size of pond.

'Joey Tomocik'.

'Lemon Mist'

Quite similar to the above with slightly paler yellow flowers and rather less strong; suitable for medium-sized ponds.

'Lemon Mist'.

'Madame Wilfron Gonnere'

Mid-pink double blooms are quite open and leaves are green; a good all-rounder.

'Madame Wilfon Gonnère'

'Marliacea Albida'

This lily makes a good alternative to *N. alba* but produces more white flowers and fewer leaves, which can have some red tinges at the edges.

'Marliacea Albida'.

'Marliacea Chromatella'

Another early Marliac selection, this superb primrose yellow lily has well marked leaves too. Suitable for medium to large ponds.

'Marliacea Chromatella'.

'Masaniello'

Rose-red flowers are cup shaped and leaves green on this useful all-round variety.

'Masaniello'.

'Marliacea Rosea'

Rather less vigorous than 'Marliacea Carnea', this variety has large pale pink flowers in good numbers, set off by green foliage.

'Marliacea Rosea'.

'Mayla'

A variety with very large, but not numerous leaves and large fuchsia-pink flowers; very elegant and suitable for larger ponds.

'Mayla'.

'Moorei'

Bred in Australia, this more recent introduction has a compact habit and is otherwise similar to Lemon Mist, with pale lemon flowers and leaves splashed with maroon markings.

'Moorei'.

'Mrs Richmond'

Supposedly the same as 'Fabiola', with strong thick tubers, green leaves and mid-pink flowers; a good variety for medium to large ponds.

'Mrs Richmond'.

'Odorata Firecrest'

Fragrant flowers with red-tipped stamens mark this variety, which is not a strong grower but good for small to medium ponds.

'Odorata Firecrest'.

'Odorata Sulphurea'

Another 'Odorata' type lily with scented flowers of sulphur yellow and leaves splashed with maroon markings, very attractive for a small to medium pond.

'Odorata Sulphurea'.

'Paul Hariot'

A changeable type lily with flowers that open yellow and darken to orange pink; good for small to medium ponds. Leaves are mostly green with small maroon flashes.

'Paul Hariot'.

'Perry's Double White'

A lovely choice for a small to medium pond, this variety has fully double pure-white flowers and olive-green foliage.

'Perry's Double White'.

'Pink Peony'

Unique peony-shaped flowers with spoon-shaped petals of soft pink held above the water among light green leaves make this one of my personal favourites.

'Pink Peony'.

'Rene Gerard'

An early selection with rosy-pink flowers with darker markings and paler outer petals.

'René Gérard'.

'Rose Arey'

Variously described as medium or large, the flowers are stellate and pale to mid-pink and the leaves green. An elegant lily.

'Rose Arey'.

'Rosennymphe'

Rather similar to Rose Arey but with larger pale pink flowers, a strong variety.

'Rosennymphe'.

'Sunrise'

This variety needs a warm and sunny position for best results, where the canary-yellow blooms will tend to come in late summer.

'Sunrise'.

'Virginalis'

Full pure white flowers grace this medium to large variety, making it an excellent substitute for N. alba and a much more attractive proposition.

'Virginalis'.

'Wanvisa'

Best new water lily in 2010, this amazing variety has flowers that are often bicolour yellow and orange and very dark purplish green leaves extensively striped and freckled in mahogany.

'Wanvisa.

'Yellow Sensation'

One of the varieties that holds on to some green leaves in all but the coldest and darkest periods, having large pale-yellow flowers with golden centres.

'Yellow Sensation'.

Large type lilies

Generally suitable for water depths of 80–100cm.

'Alba'

The only water lily native to the UK, this is a vigorous species with Marliac type rhizomes which can be as thick as your arm, producing masses of thick green leaves but relatively few medium-sized white flowers which can often be rather hidden among the pile of leaves. In most garden ponds a better result can be achieved with 'Albatross', 'Marliacea Albida' or 'Virginalis'.

Nymphaea alba.

'Arc en Ciel'

One of the varieties launched by Marliac in 1901, this produces extraordinary multi-coloured leaves marked in green, white and pink, which are more or less D-shaped. The scented flowers are stellate and white to blush pink.

'Arc en Ciel'.

'Attraction' (Marliac, 1910)

Has bright garnet to rose-red petals, paler on the outer rows. It's one of the largest reds, very good for larger ponds and a strong and reliable performer, though more susceptible to crown rot than some.

'Attraction'.

'Barbara Dobbins'

Created by Kirk Strawn in 1996, this beautiful variety has very large double peach-coloured flowers with a pink flush, which are often held above the water.

'Barbara Dobbins'.

'Charles de Meurville'

From the Marliac nursery and first offered in 1931, this has large leaves and flowers with dark pink to red outer petals, paler at the outside. It's often one of the earliest to flower.

'Charles de Meurville'.

'Colonel A.J. Welch'

An example of a viviparous lily, in which new lilies can form at the site of the old faded flowers, this pale yellow-flowering variety produces leaves prolifically.

'Colonel A.J. Welch'.

'Colossea'

Very large and thick rhizomes are typical of this white to very pale pink variety.

'Colossea'.

'Conqueror' (Marliac, 1910)

Flowers have red and pink petals with pale sepals at the outside. New leaves are purple changing to deep green.

'Conqueror'.

'Darwin'

A large lily with big double pink flowers and some of the largest green leaves on any variety; an excellent choice for large ponds and lakes.

'Darwin'.

'Escarboucle'

Meaning star, rather than carbuncle, the leaves are large but few and often almost D-shaped. The flowers are fuchsia-pink and very striking. An old variety, with poor specimens often mis-labelled, it's quite hard to find a true example now.

'Escarboucle'.

'Gladstoniana'

The biggest lily of all, with dark green leaves and huge white flowers containing a central boss of yellow stamens; a better choice than *N. alba* for larger ponds and lakes.

'Marliacea Carnea'

A strong lily with the palest pink flowers, more white with a blush really, with prolific flowers and green leaves, good for larger ponds and lakes.

'Gladstoniana'.

'Marliacea Carnea'.

'Vesuve'

Fragrant flowers of lava-red flowers are set off well by circular dark green leaves.

'Vesuve'.

CHAPTER 9

PLANTING, PROPAGATION TECHNIQUES AND POND PROBLEMS

Fortunately, water plants in general are some of the easiest plants to propagate and plant up, since one problem they don't have to deal with is desiccation of their roots; once planted they are assured of plentiful water!

PLANTING AND PROPAGATION: BASKETS AND CONTAINERS

In the UK it is standard practice to plant all marginal and submerged plants into mesh aquatic baskets, but

Aquatic plant baskets.

in most cases almost any container will do (*see* Chapter 3). The primary benefit of the mesh baskets is that the roots quickly find their way through the holes and can spread way beyond the confines of the pot, thereby gaining access to nutrients and oxygen that may have become depleted in the pot itself. Oxygen and nutrients can also migrate into the pot more easily. However, this does come with one major drawback when the time comes to re-pot them into larger containers. Because the pots are robust, the plant cannot be easily removed until all the roots growing through the meshes have been cut off flush with the pot; this will probably include nearly all of the fine terminal feeding roots. This can seem rather drastic, but actually doesn't cause any significant harm to the plant concerned, provided that it is done during the period of active growth. If new stems are emerging through the side meshes, which is common, the problem is more serious. These are of course the newest and most actively growing parts and are likely to bear the best flowers, so if you cut them all off you will be removing some of the best material (as in the picture of *Carex panicea*, overleaf, top) and leaving yourself with the older, less productive parts in the middle. This is especially the case with plants which like to spread rapidly and horizontally into new areas, such as *Butomus* (flowering rush), *Persicaria amphibia* (amphibious bistort) and many of the grasses. However,

New shoots emerging through the meshes can be lost when re-potting.

If the shoots are long enough they can be detached and used to make new plants.

if these new shoots have sufficient root attached, they can be cut off and potted up to make new plants, such as in the picture of *Baumea* (below left).

There is a further option, which is to split the original pot in several places, perhaps also cutting off the tough rim, but leaving the rest in place when repotting, thus enabling a greater proportion of the original root mass and/or side shoots to remain. Personally, I don't like doing this, but if the new stems are fleshy, such as those of *Pontederia* or *Thalia*, they can be very difficult to extract without wrecking them, and this option could be more appealing.

Many texts recommend the use of hessian to line pots with, mostly to prevent leaching of soil from inside the pot to the wider pond environment. To my mind this doesn't help much with re-potting either, since the hessian cloth bound up with the shoots and roots can make life difficult too.

Hessian pot liners

Hessian liners are often recommended to prevent soil in the pot from leaching into the pond. This came about in the early days of mesh plant pots, when the mesh size was relatively large, but modern plant pots have a much finer mesh, and the problem of leaching is much reduced. We find that the hessian cloth bound up with the shoots and roots can make life difficult when repotting, so we don't use it at our nursery, but you won't do any harm by so doing.

Hessian basket liners can be used for a 'belt and braces' job.

Sagittaria turion forming outside the pot.

Other problematic species when using mesh pots include *Sagittaria* (arrowhead). These produce small, nut-like turions at the ends of their roots, and these frequently form within the meshes of the pot, trapping and distorting them and making them impossible to remove whole. The original plant dies off at the end of the season, so if the turions are lost then that's the end of that. As a result, there are some plants that are best grown in traditional solid-sided pots with larger holes at the base. In the case of those plants that tiller sideways (*Butomus*, *Carex*, *Eriophorum*, etc.), the new shoots then come up mostly within the pot and are not compromised. The *Sagittaria* either produce the turions within the pot, or the roots travel through the larger base holes and form outside the pot completely, so these can be saved too.

However, for irises and tall plants that produce a lot of roots I still prefer the mesh baskets and the additional stability and nutrient availability that they confer. On the Continent, water lilies in particular are mostly grown in solid-sided pots, so the choice is mainly a personal one. Potted plants purchased from garden centres and mail order companies are mostly in the smaller sizes of P7, P9 and 1 litre, and these must be potted into larger pots straight away to keep them growing strongly and encourage flowering stems to be produced. I would consider a 2-litre pot to be the absolute minimum and would advise 3, 5 or even 10-litre pots for most marginal plants that are over 50cm tall when mature.

Creeping plants don't necessarily need their own dedicated pot but can be planted as an understorey in pots containing taller single-stemmed plants such as *Lythrum*. The same applies to short-lived plants that rely on seeding to keep going, such as *Myosotis* (water forget-me-not) and *Lychnis flos-cuculi* (ragged robin).

PLANTING MEDIA

So, what's the best medium in which to plant them? Of course, the answer is 'it depends'. In general, most water plants have evolved to grow in nutrient-rich silt and mud brought down from higher ground, so if you asked the plants, in most cases they would say, 'deep rich black mud in shallow water please!' However, if you are planning a natural swimming pond, you are not going to welcome clouds of black silt stirred up every time someone gets in for a dip. In this case you will be planting into clean gravel or sand, and the plants are just going to have to put up with it.

Nutrient levels

The critical thing to remember is that the aim of the game is to provide sufficient nutrients around the roots of the plants to enable them to grow and stay healthy, but to keep the dissolved nutrient concentration in the pond water as low as possible. High nutrient levels in the water will lead to unwanted algal growth, blanket weed and/or duckweed, and a murky pond.

Composts

For most garden ponds, the best medium will be either a specially formulated aquatic soil, bagged soil-based compost of some kind, or garden soil, or a mixture of the above. At my nursery we use almost exclusively either good Devon topsoil (for any submerged plants like water lilies) or aquatic compost and sterile John Innes type compost mixed with municipal recycled compost and fine gravel in various ratios for marginal plants. The only reason that we buy sterile bagged compost for marginals is to avoid the chore of weeding that results from using as-dug soil from the land; in other respects the latter would be ideal. Standard multipurpose compost isn't any use for marginal plants in mesh pots, since it dissolves readily and disappears from the pots; it's also lighter than water and not heavy enough to make the planted pots stable when placed in the water. It's only used for propagation in the early stages, such as striking cuttings and seed sowing. The bagged aquatic soils have improved significantly over the years but are still expensive considering that most contain a high proportion of grit and sand. They vary quite a lot in terms of their density and nutrient content too.

Fertiliser

Aquatic plants are fast growing and therefore require a lot of nutrients, which is contradictory to the use of low nutrient soils in which to grow them. If you do buy low-nutrient aquatic compost you will almost certainly need to add fertiliser sooner rather than later, which rather defeats the object. So, how do you know when you need to add fertiliser, and what should you use?

The most convenient format is a slow-release tablet such as Osmocote. These sometimes weigh 5g, or more usually 7.5g, and can be added at the rate of one to three tablets per 3 litres of pot size at the beginning of the season, thereby steadily providing feed just where it is needed, at the roots, for the whole season. Even in the low nutrient systems required for natural swimming pools, slow-release tablets are frequently necessary to keep water lilies and tall architectural plants like *Pontederia* looking green and lush. Don't

Fertiliser tablets will make a tremendous difference to the performance of your lily.

ever use fertiliser during the autumn or winter months as it won't be used by the plants and will slowly dissolve into the pond water, encouraging algal growth.

Lastly, it is worth topping the planted pots with a layer of gravel or grit to reduce the amount of nutrients leaching from the soil surface into the water and give a pleasing neat surface. Avoid limestone grit or broken slate, which can raise the pH; flint or granite pea gravel is best.

PROPAGATION

Many water plants are very simple to propagate. Naturally, any that produce seeds can be grown by germinating their seeds.

Growing from seed

Please be aware that named varieties mostly don't come true from seed but will produce offspring that look generally similar to their parents. Most seeds germinate best if they are harvested and sown immediately before they dry out completely, though some may need one or more periods of frost to break their dormancy. Large seeds such as those produced by *Irises* and *Thalia* are the most reliable, but some dust-like seeds, such as those of *Mimulus ringens*, can be tricky to collect and handle. Some plants produce so many seeds that they are frankly a wretched nuisance, such as *Carex pendula*, *Cyperus eragrostis* and *Mimulus guttatus*. In these cases, it's not a question of making more but weeding out the excess. Others produce many seeds but relatively few plants result naturally, such as *Caltha* (marsh marigold), *Lychnis flos-cuculi* (ragged robin) and *Myosotis* (water forget-me-not), but if the seeds are collected or seedlings are pricked out, a very large number can be created from just one parent plant.

The main hurdles when growing water plants from seed is the propensity for liverworts to grow on the surface of the compost and swamp the seedlings, or for the young seedlings to be grazed off by slugs and snails. As ever, seeds do best sown not too thickly and not too deeply. One of the most reliable techniques is to mix grit and compost about 70/30 in a shallow tray and compact very lightly with a flat board. Mix finer seeds with a little dry sand and spread thinly and evenly across the surface. Shake some very fine grit or sand over the

Stand the seed tray inside another, larger, water-filled tray to keep slugs and snails off.

top, hardly covering them, and compact very lightly once more. Stand the whole seed tray in a larger tray of very shallow water with the soil surface above water level (this will keep the compost saturated and stop slugs and snails getting access) and place the whole in a warm, well-lit place. Check regularly for trouble and pot up seedlings when they are big enough to handle. They may well not germinate until the following Spring.

However, there are many other techniques to multiply water plants quickly and easily.

Rooting stems

Lots of water plants will produce roots on horizontal stems, which can then be detached and planted up as new plants. Examples are *Lysimachia nummularia* (creeping Jenny), *Mentha* (water mint), and *Veronica beccabunga* (brooklime).

Others can be propagated by lying previously upright stems horizontally in water; these will produce

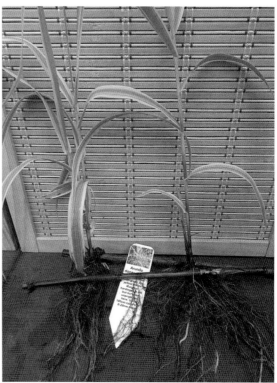

Laying woody stems in water can encourage the plant to produce new roots and stems at the leaf node.

Many creeping plants produce roots at the leaf nodes.

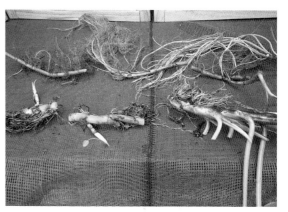

Stems that are segmented can often simply be cut into pieces and floated to produce new plants.

roots and shoots at the nodes and can then be cut into sections and potted up. They include *Arundo* (giant water reed), *Mimulus ringens* (blue monkey musk), *Scrophularia* (figwort) and many others. Some that have segmented horizontal stems, like *Acorus*, *Calla* and *Menyanthes* can simply be divided into lengths and sprouted by floating in water.

Cuttings

Cuttings may be taken of ripe or semi-ripe stems during the growing season from such subjects as *Lythrum* (loosestrife) and *Potentilla* (marsh cinquefoil); these can be bunched together in a mesh pot filled with grit and placed in warm shallow water until rooted, then split up and potted on.

Division

Lastly, there is the method of simple division, which works for just about everything. When pots become overfull and congested, simply cut the root ball into sections using a heavy knife, secateurs, or a mallet and cleaver for tough old things like *Carex* and *Thalia* that have become inextricably bound up in a tough plastic pot. You can be absolutely brutal with most water plants and it's not difficult to produce half a dozen or more good plants from a single overgrown pot. This is the only way to ensure that named varieties remain true. The image here shows a *Thalia* which has out-grown its pot, leaves are starting to go yellow and the plant has become top heavy and prone to topple. Start by cutting off all the roots projecting through the pot and remove the pot. Now cut back all the top growth to good shoots low down. Insert a heavy knife and cut downwards, trying not to sever shoots near their base and retaining a portion of root on each section. After dividing, tidy up any crushed or damaged stems or

Bunches of cuttings can be stood in water in a perforated pot to produce multiple new plants.

This *Thalia* is starting to look a bit yellow and the pot is bursting with material – time to re-pot.

First cut off all the roots projecting through the basket.

Wash off excess soil, exposing new shoots, and cut back older stems.

Then knock out of the basket.

Divide into sections, each with at least one strong shoot and some roots.

roots to reduce the risk of fungal or bacterial infection.

Pot up all the divisions into fresh compost and when strong new growth begins, push in one or two fertiliser tablets. With many plants such as *Caltha*, *Primula* and *Ranunculus* it's best not to over-divide into individual

Re-pot the sections into fresh compost with a fertiliser tablet in each. Top the pot with clean gravel.

plants but keep them as small clumps; they seem to like being with their mates and get going much more quickly.

POND PROBLEMS

Fortunately, aquatic plants suffer from relatively few ailments, and those that exist tend to be fairly host specific, but there are a few to be aware of. Well-fed plants grown in conditions that suit them are rarely badly affected, but as ever, vigilance and prompt action are key.

Fungi: moulds, rusts, mildews, etc.

These primitive and ubiquitous organisms are principally agents of decay, affecting mostly tissue which is already damaged or necrotic, but they can also affect live tissue, especially if the host plant is under stress such as drought or excessive heat. On a garden scale,

treatment with fungicides is not generally recommended, since the problem tends to be seasonal and does little long-term damage.

Alisma *smut fungus*

This causes black patches on the leaves of all species of *Alisma*, but particularly the native species *Alisma plantago* and the American *A. subcordatum (parviflorum)*. There's nothing much to be done about it, but it does tend to affect plants only after flowering and seems not to confer long-lasting damage. Similar fungi affect the leaves of *Caltha* and *Filipendula* after flowering; these should be trimmed off whereupon new unaffected leaves will emerge. Fungicide treatment is not recommended.

Mildew

Mildews often affect the leaves, crowns and roots of plants after flowering; this is normal and unlikely to cause lasting damage. Particularly susceptible genera include *Ranunculus*, (especially *R. flammula*), *Filipendula* (especially *F. ulmaria*), *Caltha*, and *Primula*. Trim off affected foliage and ensure that plants have not dried out. In particularly bad cases affecting the roots, a fungicide drench can be used, but such treatment is not normally necessary.

Rusts

This family of fungi manifests itself as brown spotting, streaking or dusting on the leaves of many plants,

Mildew on *Caltha* leaf after flowering.

usually as a result of drought stress but often as a result of the natural die-back of old foliage. It's very common on grasses and extends to other plants with blade-like leaves such as irises, also *Lythrum salicaria* and *Persicaria amphibia*. Almost all water irises are somewhat affected after flowering, as are *Acorus*, *Carex* and *Cyperus* genera. It can affect almost any plant but again, treatment is not generally required, as the disease is seasonal and does not damage the plants permanently. Simply cut back affected leaves.

Root rots

These can be caused by various families of fungi including *Phytophthora* and *Pythium*. Once these take hold they can spread into live healthy tissue and prompt action is necessary to prevent this. The most likely way for them to gain a hold is when plants have been split or moved and physical damage to roots has occurred, especially when temperatures are low. The best advice is to leave plants unmolested in winter and only divide when in active growth, when the plants' natural defences are active too. Unfortunately, it has become common practice for many larger growers to give regular fungicide treatments in an attempt to control these infections in commercial crops; this has meant that resistance has become quite a problem with some varieties. *Iris laevigata* and *Iris louisiana* varieties seem particularly susceptible. The kinds of fungicides available to the general public are unlikely to resolve these problems and the best course with individual plants is to remove them and dispose of them, not composting them.

Bacteria

Bacteria are ubiquitous but rarely cause problems with healthy plants. However, if the plants are stressed by adverse growing conditions, bacteria can infect leaves and roots. One example would be bacterial leaf spotting on water lilies. Water lilies prefer a higher pH than neutral, but if they are grown under acidic conditions, it is quite likely that red or brown spots will appear on the leaves. These are mostly cosmetic, and the plant as a whole may be relatively unaffected. Water lily crown rot is an extreme example of bacterial infection and will cause complete breakdown of the crown, preceded by yellowing of leaves and their detachment from the crown. There is no cure for this, and some varieties seem much more affected than others. Plants that recover can perpetuate the infection. Lilies are much more susceptible if summer temperatures are not high enough. No treatment is possible, and any suspect plants should be completely removed and not composted.

Aphids

These sap-sucking insects can affect very many plants and can be vectors for subsequent bacterial or fungal infection. Fortunately, they don't affect many water plants and can be fairly easily dealt with. The most susceptible plants are those with succulent leaves like *Alisma*, *Sagittaria* and *Pontederia*. If the plants are hosed off with a forceful spray, most of the aphids will be dislodged and fall into the water. The majority can be netted off with a fine meshed pond net, and the remainder can be predated by backswimmers, pond skaters and other insects and amphibians. Water lilies have their own species of aphid (*Rhopalosiphum nymphaeae*) which make the leaves look like they have been dusted with pepper from a pepper mill, before yellowing and dying. Proprietary aphid sprays are also effective but need to be used with special care in an aquatic environment in case they affect beneficial species. Majestik is a readily available organic approved non-toxic wax-based compound that can be effective. When sprayed to run-off, it blocks the tiny breathing holes in the aphids' bodies. However, it can affect beneficial species too.

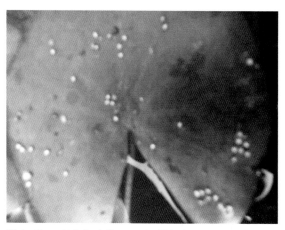

Water lily aphids look like cracked black pepper on the leaves.

China mark moth (*Elophila nymphaeata*)

This is an incredible insect, the caterpillars of which manufacture their own little boat or 'quiver' from pieces of the water lily leaves. They use these to migrate from leaf to leaf, cutting out tell-tale oval pieces. They are voracious and can devastate a lily patch in short order. New leaves will continue to be provided by the plant, but unless the infestation is dealt with the lily can become exhausted and die. A miracle of nature, but one which may be hard to appreciate if it is your prize water lily that is the prey. Their quivers protect them from most insecticidal sprays, but a level of biological control can be achieved using BT (*Bacillus thuringiensis*), a bacterium which infects caterpillars' intestinal tracts. I have found this very effective.

Water lily beetle (*Galerucella nymphaeae*)

This beetle can be devastating for water lilies, feeding on the leaves and leaving characteristic track marks where the surface of the leaf has been grazed off. The beetles themselves are hard to find; it is the monumental amounts of poo that they leave behind which are obvious. They are difficult to remove by hosing off and best treated with soft soap or a non-toxic oil or wax-based spray such as Majestik. Despite being non-toxic and often organically-approved, these sprays work by blocking the breathing apparatus of insects and so are not specific to pests, and can kill beneficial species too.

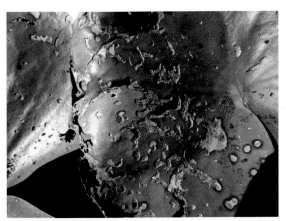

Water lily beetles mine into the leaves, causing a lot of damage.

Snails

There are various species of pond snail, including the great pond snail *Limnaea stagnalis* and the ramshorn snails *Planorbarius corneus* and *P. planorbis*. Legend has it that the latter two are less damaging to plants than the former, but I think that is mostly racial discrimination because the ramshorn snails are prettier. It is certainly true that *Limnaea* can devastate *Aponogeton* (water hawthorn), but all snails graze algae and in so doing damage the leaf surface, so it's probably best to tolerate small numbers but thin out any excess. If you see damaged plants together with a high number of snails, it's probably not a coincidence.

Pond snails can damage leaves while grazing algae.

Mice and voles

Both can be destructive to certain types of plants. In our nursery they think they are little beavers and run around felling the stems of horsetails especially, leaving them in neat piles of mini logs. Anything grassy with stiff thin stems seems to be a target and *Rhynchospora* (*Dichromena*) is another favourite. They can also get into the heart of *Gunnera* during winter and eat it out like Swiss cheese when they get the urge.

Unwanted plants

Weeds of one kind or another are far more likely to give you grief than the problems above. By far the biggest culprits are the algae.

Algae

Algae fall into two main camps: the unicellular free-floating type, which cause 'pea soup' that can shade the bottom-dwelling plants to such an extent that they die out, and the string algae (blanket weed), like green cotton wool, which smothers everything under the water and clogs up the whole pond. There is a further group of rooted algae such as the stoneworts typified by *Chara* and *Nitella* genera, but these cause relatively few difficulties and are characteristic of clear water. They can build up to nuisance proportions and smother the new leaves of water lilies, but this is relatively unusual.

'Pea soup' is often one of the first stages of progression once a new pond has been built and stocked with plants and/or fish and is very likely to occur if there are a significant number of fish in the pond being regularly fed on artificial food. These organisms are at the very bottom of the food chain and are absolutely essential for life. They make use of sunlight and free dissolved nutrients in the water and can reproduce incredibly rapidly. This is a natural process and unless the situation is prolonged and unchanging, it does not necessitate any action, since the normal chain of events is for zooplankton to miraculously appear and increase rapidly to eat the algae until their own population can no longer be sustained by the food source and they die off, releasing nutrients back into the water, after which the cycle repeats itself until a balance is achieved.

'Blanket weed' is quite another matter. The cause is exactly the same, which is to say an excess of dissolved nutrients in the water, particularly phosphates and nitrates. Blanket weed also thrives in disturbed water and tends to be much worse in ponds containing waterfalls, airstones or other turbulent flow. Certain minerals such as the phosphate family are particularly likely to encourage algal growth if present in even tiny concentrations. Also, algal growth is much more likely in hard water than in soft water. Unfortunately, most mains tap water in the UK is likely to be quite high or very high in phosphates, so these can be introduced in excess with an initial tap water fill-up (hence the often-repeated advice to fill up with collected rainwater if possible). Until this excess has been taken up by plant growth there is a significant likelihood that blanket weed will be a problem. So, what can be done about it? Aside from using soft water to fill the pond if possible, to minimise the phosphate and nitrate introduction in the first place, various courses of action are possible:

1. Manual removal. By using a broom with long bristles, it is possible to remove the worst of the material that is in the open water, but if the blanket weed has smothered plants like oxygenators growing below the surface, it can be very difficult to remove without removing all the oxygenators too. Nevertheless, a routine of regularly removing the excess is a good way to remove the nutrients from the system. Some species are undoubtedly much easier to deal with than others; the coarse net-like strands of *Cladophora* can be wound up around a wooden broom handle and almost every scrap picked up, but the slimy and gloopy clumps of *Spirogyra* break into innumerable loose strands when disturbed and are best removed by careful siphoning. Of course, if the water siphoned out with it is replaced by more of the high nutrient or hard tap water, the problem will simply be perpetuated. Many pond keepers agonise over the myriad creatures which are inadvertently caught up in the removal process, but you simply can't save every one. Note, however, that this proves that some algae can be beneficial to a number of creatures. Just give them a chance to escape and crawl back in by leaving the extracted algae close to the pond overnight before taking it completely away.

2. Natural remedies. Barley straw placed loosely in nets within the pond seems to help in many cases. The method of action is rather obscure, but it is generally accepted that micro-organisms growing in the decomposing straw somehow compete for the nutrients causing the algae and

Blanket weed forms in ponds containing high nutrient levels.

reduce its severity. There may also be allelopathic compounds released during decomposition that reduce the growth rate of the algae. There are many products on the market which claim to make use of these qualities but there is little hard evidence for a quick result. Other products based on peroxides claim to kill off algae by a strong oxidation reaction; however, these products can affect other submerged foliage too. I am naturally averse to using any chemical product which does not clearly state its content or method of action.

3. Pond dye. Several companies manufacture a non-toxic dye that blocks the wavelengths of light needed by the algae for photosynthesis. It's mostly used in fishing ponds which are required to stay clear, ponds for swimming, or ponds which look like a dark mirror in formal gardens. It only works well at depths over a metre, so is of limited use in garden ponds, and is non-specific, therefore affects oxygenators and other submerged plants too.

4. Ultrasound. Some authors claim that high frequency sound generators can disrupt algal cells while not affecting higher plants, but again this technique has little hard evidence in its favour.

5. Competition. Blanket weed problems are mostly symptomatic of new ponds, or those with a high input of nutrients, where a balanced ecosystem has not developed. There is no doubt that a well-planted pond will in time suffer much less of a problem, provided that excess nutrients are not allowed to remain in the system. Plants with floating leaves, or rafting plants, which shade the surface of the pond, are particularly helpful. Other plants will compete with the algae and prevent its excessive growth – don't forget that even algae are necessary in a complete ecosystem, and it is not practical or desirable to eliminate any single component. Remember that nutrients are only permanently removed from the system when plant material or sludge is removed, often in autumn, and a significant extra nutrient load arrives in winter in the form of fallen leaves and nutrient-rich surface water from surrounding soil.

Pond problems.

shadier environment and is rarely a problem in large open ponds. There are three common species that mostly float, namely *Lemna minor* (common duckweed), *L. gibba* (fat duckweed) and *L. polyrrhiza*, and one that mostly lives under water, *L. trisulca* (ivy-leaved duckweed). *L. minor* is the one which causes most of the problems and can quickly cover the water surface, denying light to submerged plants such as oxygenators. All overwinter as microscopic buds or turions on the pond bottom and among submerged foliage, floating to the surface in spring and reproducing rapidly. It is impractical to prevent duckweed from arriving (I'm sure it comes down with rain), but the best way to control it is to remove the excess manually and religiously, keep the dissolved nutrient levels low and site the pond in full sun. One of the few advantages to having a few goldfish about is that they will mop up a small quantity too. If you have an intractable duckweed problem, you must attend to the underlying cause before you have any hope of getting the situation under control. There are reports that the native brooklime (*Veronica beccabunga*) produces an allelopathic substance which deters duckweed; this may be so, but I have not observed it. I think my duckweed is made of sterner stuff.

Other weeds

Many aquatic plants, especially those which have evolved to rapidly colonise new areas, can be problematic weeds in their own right. They can arrive in the pond as a result of an ill-judged decision at the

Duckweed

This pesky little plant is a nuisance in ponds with a high nutrient content, but unlike algae will do better in a

Azolla (fairy moss) is still a problem in many ponds despite having been banned for years.

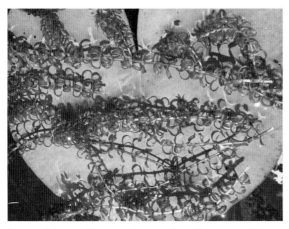

Lagarosiphon major can out-compete native oxygenators.

Crassula (swamp stonecrop) is another almost ineradicable pest.

planting stage, as seeds or seedlings hidden among other plants or from the nearby environment. If your neighbour has a pond crammed full of such nuisance plants, then you can bet it won't be too long before your pond is affected too. There's no substitute for vigilance and regular weeding and the very best advice is to research the plants you have chosen and avoid any that are likely to cause problems. You should also look upon gifts from other pond keepers with great suspicion and quarantine them for a good length of time before moving them to your pond. The ones to be really scrupulous about are the ones that have been banned from sale but still continue to pop up their cheery heads everywhere, such as *Azolla* (fairy moss), *Crassula* (swamp stonecrop) and *Lagarosiphon* (curly pond weed).

Wildfowl

Almost everybody is delighted when Mrs Mallard first appears, especially if she brings her young family of gorgeous ducklings. However, while ducks can certainly be welcome on larger ponds, they can be quite a nuisance in small ones, especially as they grow and if there are several of them. The novelty is apt to wear off after a few days, when all the floating plants have been eaten, the pond and its surroundings have a generous layer of slimy duck poop and everything that hasn't been eaten has been trampled flat or knocked off the shelf into the bottom of the pond! If you do keep ducks, it's best to give them their own pond to trash and keep them fenced away from your garden pond. The situation is a hundred times worse if Canada geese decide to honour you with a visit, and even in quite large ponds these birds are frankly a menace. They are most damaging when they arrive shortly after a pond has been planted, whereupon they will pull up all the plants they can reach, picking off the tenderest leaves

Ducks are delightful, but not in large numbers.

problems in the bud. This is the best time of year to attend to a tidy-up since most of the wildlife has finished breeding, amphibians have mostly left the pond and the herbaceous plants are going dormant with browning leaves and stems.

Handy tip

Before you start stirring up the mud by climbing in and out, bail some clean pond water into several containers. You can place any animals that you come across into this clean water, rather than blocking their gills in a bucket of sludge which is all that is available towards the end of the job.

and leaving the rest high and dry on the bank or float-ing around the pond. If you are planning a large pond, it's best to avoid planting in spring when the geese are looking for nesting sites, but plant in autumn when they are starting to disappear, and the cut-back, browning foliage is less attractive to them. If you're thinking about incorporating an island into your larger pond, please be aware that an island is the most desir-able piece of goose real estate of all.

POND AFTERCARE

While it's true to say that a decent-sized wildlife pond needs relatively little attention, when compared to a herbaceous border, it is not a maintenance-free envi-ronment. A pond tends to look its best between three and five years after creation and planting, but if left to its own devices will deteriorate thereafter as the silt and debris within the pond builds up and the most vigorous plants start to out-compete the weaker ones. The pond pictured in the section on algae is reaching that point (*see* page 185). The reed mace and flag iris are making a bid for world domination and the blanket weed is building up, a sure sign that there is a lot of organic material on the bottom causing an enriched environment. *Typha latifolia* is a nitrogen fixer and will steadily increase the nitrogen levels, exacerbating the problem.

It's not necessary to keep a pond as clean and ordered as an operating theatre, but a little attention, especially in autumn, is well worthwhile to nip developing

A little silt on the bottom is not a problem, but a thick layer of rotting leaves and vegetation will enrich the environment, causing anaerobic conditions, pro-ducing toxic gases and poisoning the water. Remove the excess, leaving as much as you can temporarily close enough to the pond that any remaining animals have at least some chance of getting back. Cut back all herbaceous plants to 5 to 10cm above the pot, but not to below water level, as water can enter hollow stems and cause a rot inside the plant. Remove excess rampant plants and repot those that need it but, if possible, leave any plants that need dividing until spring. If you haven't removed too much of the origi-nal pond water, don't top up with tap water since the winter rain will do that job for you and be better for the pond.

Remember, removing organic matter from the pond regularly is the only way to permanently remove nutrients from the system, otherwise they just get recycled, and the pond will become more and more fertile and eutrophic, increasing problems with unwanted algal growth.

LINER REPAIRS

It may be that at some point you notice that the water level is lower than expected and you discover that there must be a hole in your pond liner. Such holes are notoriously hard to find, but if you wait until the water level stabilises it follows that the hole is at water level. Once you find it, take out a few more buckets full of water and clean and dry the affected area before patching. Patching kits are available for most liners, and these work well on newish material, but it can be much harder with old liner that has gone brittle and inflexible, especially the cheaper, thinner grades. These days one of the waterproof do-all glues or sealants will usually effect a seal, but in my experience this can be short-lived.

This might be a good time to cover the issue of sharp plant roots. Some pond plants do undoubtedly have sharp root tips, or more commonly shoot tips, and some people worry a great deal about this. However, such shoots grow mostly vertically upwards, so the risk of a puncture downwards is small. It's possible that roots or shoots could travel into a fold in the liner and penetrate it, but it's a small risk and is likely to self-seal as the root or shoot expands. It's much more likely to develop into a problem when you decide to heave out the plant for some maintenance, so take care when doing this. The pond baskets themselves are quite sharp when broken or split too, so take care to lift them rather than drag them. A good practice is to stand pond baskets on an old roofing slate on top of a doubled liner offcut, though slates can have sharp edges too! Given the difficulty of tracing and fixing leaks in a flexible liner, and the low cost of a new one, the most pragmatic solution is often to leave the old one *in situ* and simply fit a new liner inside it. This may of course involve lifting and re-setting any surrounding edge paving or turf.

KEY
1. Pond skater Gerris lacustris.
2. Great diving beetle Dytiscus marginalis.
3. Greater water boatman Notonecta glauca.
4. Water hoglouse Asellus aquaticus.
5. Freshwater shrimp Gammarus pulex.
6. Dragonfly larva Anisoptera sp.
7. Great crested newt Triturus cristatus.

CHAPTER 10

INTEGRATING THE POND WITH THE SURROUNDING AREA

One of the factors that turn a good pond into an excellent one is the way in which it is integrated into its surroundings. A major hurdle in the way of achieving this in most garden ponds is the capillary barrier formed by the pond liner. It's a common misconception that because a pond is full of water, the area immediately next to the pond is therefore a suitable place to plant moisture loving plants. Of course, when you stop to think about it, any liner prevents water from escaping, and the fact that you have excavated a hole means that any surface water drains even more readily than before, following the underside of the liner and draining away. Thus, the area immediately outside the pond may actually be even drier than other places in the same garden. At the edges of a natural pond, the soil will remain damp as a result of capillary action, but in a lined pond the liner is a barrier to capillary movement of water (see Chapter 1).

There are two ways in which this anomaly can be overcome. Firstly, one can choose to use plants which look similar to the aquatic plants in the pond but require drier conditions. For example, *Liatris* looks similar to *Lythrum*, and border irises replicate the look of aquatic ones. By creating associations such as these, the look of the pond planting can be extended beyond the boundaries of the pond itself without having to create special conditions for the plants.

Secondly, one can create artificially damp conditions outside of the pond perimeter in order to use the same families that would colonise this area in a natural situation; this is harder than it may seem if one is not simply to duplicate conditions in the margin of the pond. This is a subject which was visited before in Chapter 5 but stands repeating here. Many plants thought of as 'bog' plants or even sold with the prefix 'bog', such as 'bog' primulas or 'bog' sage will generally not thrive in squelchy wet, boggy conditions, especially in winter and even more so in cold areas. This goes for all the leafy moisture-loving plants such as *Astilbe*, *Ligularia*, *Rodgersia*, *Trollius* and the wide range of candelabra primulas, all often referred to as 'bog' plants. So, one needs to provide very special conditions for these plants, which are rarely found naturally in gardens.

This can be done either by using a separate liner to form the underground reservoir, or by extending the pond liner right under the area intended for moisture-loving plants, in which case the pond water itself will be contiguous with the reservoir. In the former case, a length of 110mm plastic drainpipe set vertically in one corner will allow the water level in the reservoir to be monitored during dry spells and topped up as necessary. The top 15–30cm of soil should be a mixture of 30–50 per cent grit and 50–70 per cent loam, to create

An integrated planting scheme ensures a seamless transition from water to land.

Moisture-loving plants.

Making a damp garden

It's commonly suggested that in order to create an area for damp-loving plants next to a pond, one should line a hole with a sheet of plastic or old pond liner and stab it over with a fork to 'allow some drainage'. Sadly, this is highly unlikely to achieve the desired result. What you will have created is essentially a giant plant pot. In winter the drainage will be insufficient to prevent the soil from becoming totally saturated, and in summer the soil within the liner will be cut off from the surrounding soil by the liner and therefore unable to draw on the surrounding area for moisture.

The key thing to remember is that you are trying to prevent the soil from ever becoming totally saturated, but also to prevent it from completely drying out. This is achieved by creating a low-level reservoir, well below the crown of the plants, which allows water to rise by capillary action as needed, and an upper level of well-drained, open soil in which most of the roots of the plants will be found.

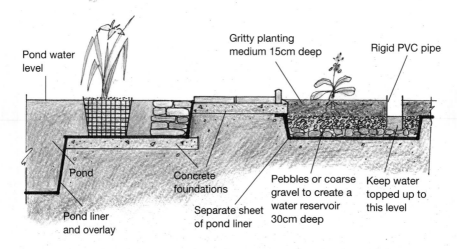

Section of pond showing area for moisture-loving plants.

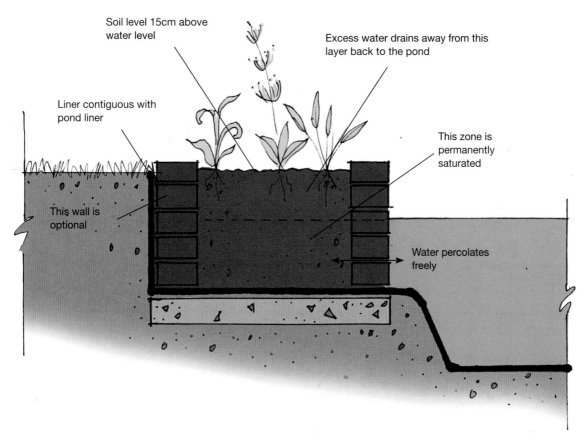

Soil level 15cm above
water level

Excess water drains away from this
layer back to the pond

Liner contiguous with
pond liner

This zone is
permanently
saturated

This wall is
optional

Water percolates
freely

Liner contiguous under adjacent damp garden.

a rich, well-drained but permanently moist planting zone. Whichever method is used, the planting can then be extended and eventually merged with the wider garden planting in a seamless and natural way.

The damp soil edges of a natural pond can be quite difficult to maintain, since weeds will germinate easily and grow strongly in such ideal conditions. Tough grasses in particular can penetrate well into the marginal planting and are then very hard to control. Apart from many hours spent weeding manually, there is little to be done about this, but it does help to have a protruding, hard and impenetrable edging material such as timber or Corten steel at the interface between the marginal planting and whatever is beyond. It's then easier to concentrate on keeping the strip immediately inside the edge weed free. A regularly mown grass strip around the pond allows easy access and keeps other weeds to a minimum and an occasional pass with a line strimmer helps to tidy up any wayward seed heads.

If the area adjacent to the pond is being grazed by animals, it is likely that a lot of trampling and muddy edges will result, so this is not usually satisfactory except in larger and wilder ponds. Fortunately, most terrestrial weeds don't fare well further out and peter out in more than a few centimetres of water.

WILDLIFE IN THE POND

Within minutes of filling your pond with water it is possible to witness the first pioneers checking out the new real estate. Often, it's the more colourful flying insects that will be most obvious; dragonflies and damselflies will immediately start to investigate and attempt to establish their new territory. Smaller insects such as water boatmen and pond skaters can fly too but may not be so obvious at first. The biggest and mostly accidental new wave of animals will arrive with the first

The fierce creatures living in your pond. Author's note: this original artwork by Hester Aspland is based on a photo I took at my nursery of two dragonfly larvae attacking a dead newt, like a pair of medieval warriors, or two sharks attacking a whale carcass. It's a tough environment and only the strong survive!

A selection of pond creatures.

Ramshorn and common pond snails.

plants to be re-homed in your pond. Whether these have come from the garden centre, in the post or from a friend, the plant material will be full of eggs and insects in all stages of growth, even tadpoles and young newts. It's remarkable how a previously unoccupied volume of water can suddenly be home to dozens of different species.

Establishment of a balanced ecosystem

It takes some time for a balanced ecosystem to become established, but there is a typical progression which goes something like this:

- The first plants to appear, other than those deliberately introduced, will be the algae. Unicellular or basic multicellular algae will be present in the fill-up water, rainwater and soil and plants around the pond and will begin to multiply, changing the water from clear to cloudy in varying degrees, initially depending mainly on temperature and the availability of dissolved nutrients in the water.

- Once the algae are sufficiently numerous, zooplankton such as *Daphnia* will miraculously appear and start to feed on the algae. As the algae are mopped up, the water will clear once more, but eventually there will be insufficient algae for the burgeoning population of zooplankton and the latter will die off, leaving behind resistant eggs among the plants and silt forming on the bottom of the pond. As their bodies die and decay, the zooplankton release nutrients back into the water, feeding another cycle of algal growth and a further zooplankton bloom when the eggs hatch. This process repeats itself many times but eventually

Dragonfly on *Typha* flower.

the peaks and troughs become less marked, and an equilibrium begins to develop.

- Detritus feeders such as water hoglice and freshwater shrimps will start to consume the organic material left behind. Concurrently, larger insects such as water boatmen [3] and pond skaters [1] will arrive and more complex algae such as *Chara*, *Nitella* and *Spirogyra* will begin to develop.
- Local populations of frogs, toads and newts [7] will join the queue of wildlife investigating the pond and some will take up residence. Small mammals and reptiles will use the pond for drinking water and will start to hunt the increasing supply of insects and amphibians, and eventually apex predators like foxes and otters may take advantage of the small mammals and amphibians.

Here are some of the more interesting pond residents and visitors to look out for:

- Plankton: water flea (*Daphnia*), *Cyclops*.

Orange tip butterfly on *Peltiphyllum* flower.

Succisa pratensis attracts many pollinators.

- Surface insects: whirligig beetles (*Gyrinus* spp.), pond skaters (*Gerris lacustris*) [1], water measurers (*Hydrometra stagnorum*), water stick insects (*Ranatra linearis*).
- Sub-surface insects: greater and lesser water boatmen (*Notonecta glauca* [3] and *Corixa punctata* respectively), larvae of dragonflies [6] (*Anisoptera*) and damselflies (*Zygoptera*) of many species, stoneflies (*Plecoptera*), alderflies (*Sialidae*), mayflies (*Ephemeroptera*) and caddis flies (Trichoptera), water scorpion (*Nepa cinerea*), great diving beetles (*Dytiscus marginalis*) [2], freshwater shrimps (*Gammarus pulex*) [5], water hoglice (*Asellus aquaticus*) [4].
- Molluscs: great pond snail (*Limnaea stagnalis*), ramshorn snail (*Planorbis* spp.).
- Amphibians and reptiles: great crested [7], smooth and palmate newts (*Triturus* spp.), common frogs (*Rana* spp.) and toads (*Bufo* spp.), grass snakes.
- Insects in flight: dragonflies and damselflies, butterflies, hoverflies, wasps and bees.

APPENDIX I: LATIN NAMES AND COMMON NAME EQUIVALENTS

Latin Name	Common Name(s)
Acorus calamus	Sweet flag
Acorus gramineus cvs	Japanese sweet flag
Alisma spp.	Water plantain
Anagallis	Bog pimpernel
Anemopsis	Yerba mansa, Apache beads
Aponogeton	Water hawthorn
Astilbe	False goat's beard
Baldellia spp.	Lesser water plantain
Baumea	Golden spear, variegated rush
Butomus cvs	Flowering rush
Calla	Bog arum
Callitriche	Starwort
Caltha	Marsh marigold, kingcup
Carex spp.	Sedges
Ceratophyllum	Hornwort
Cyperus longus	Galingale
Cyperus cvs	Umbrella grass
Equisetum	Horsetail
Eleocharis	Spike-rush
Eriophorum	Cotton grass
Filipendula	Meadowsweet
Fontinalis antipyretica	Willow moss
Geum	Water avens
Gratiola	Water hyssop
Gunnera	Giant rhubarb, Brazilian rhubarb
Hippuris vulgaris	Marestail
Hottonia	Water violet

Latin Name	Common Name(s)
Houttuynia	Chameleon plant
Iris pseudacorus	Yellow flag
Iris versicolor	Blue flag
Juncus effusus	Soft rush
Juncus effusus spiralis	Corkscrew rush
Juncus inflexus	Hard rush
Justicia	Water willow
Lychnis flos-cuculi	Ragged robin
Lysimachia nummularia	Creeping Jenny
Lysimachia punctata	Dotted loosestrife, yellow loosestrife
Lysimachia vulgaris	Yellow loosestrife
Lythrum spp.	Purple loosestrife
Mentha aquatica	Water mint
Mentha cervina	Water spearmint
Mentha pulegium	Pennyroyal
Myriophyllum spp.	Milfoils
Nasturtium aquaticum	Watercress
Nuphar spp.	Brandy bottles
Nymphaea cvs	Water lilies
Nymphoides peltata	Fringe lily, water fringe
Orontium	Golden club
Peltandra	Arrow arum
Persicaria amphibia	Amphibious bistort
Phalaris	Reed canary grass
Phragmites	Norfolk reed

Latin Name	Common Name(s)
Phyla	Frog fruit
Pontederia	Pickerel weed
Potamogeton natans	Broad-leaved pondweed
Ranunculus aquatilis	Water crowfoot
Ranunculus flammula	Lesser spearwort
Ranunculus hederaceus	Ivy-leaved crowfoot
Ranunculus lingua	Greater spearwort
Rumex spp.	Docks
Sagittaria spp.	Arrowheads

Latin Name	Common Name(s)
Salvia uliginosa	Bog sage
Saururus	Lizard's tail
Schoenoplectus	Bulrush
Scirpus	Needle spike-rush
Stachys palustris	Marsh woundwort
Thalia	Alligator flag
Typha	Reed mace, bulrush
Veronica beccabunga	Brooklime
Zantedeschia	Arum lily

APPENDIX II: COMMON NAMES AND LATIN NAME EQUIVALENTS

Common Name(s)	Latin Name
Alligator flag	*Thalia dealbata*
Amphibious bistort	*Persicaria amphibia*
Arrow arum	*Peltandra*
Arrowheads	*Sagittaria* spp.
Arum lily	*Zantedeschia*
Blue flag	*Iris versicolor*
Bog arum	*Calla palustris*
Bog pimpernel	*Anagallis tenella*
Bog sage	*Salvia uliginosa*
Brandy bottle	*Nuphar lutea*
Broad-leaved pondweed	*Potamogeton natans*
Brooklime	*Veronica beccabunga*

Common Name(s)	Latin Name
Bulrush	*Schoenoplectus lacustris*
Chameleon plant	*Houttuynia cordata*
Corkscrew rush	*Juncus effusus spiralis*
Cotton grass	*Eriophorum* spp.
Creeping Jenny	*Lysimachia nummularia*
Docks	*Rumex* spp.
Dotted loosestrife, yellow loosestrife	*Lysimachia punctata*
False goat's beard	*Astilbe* spp.
Flowering rush	*Butomus umbellatus*
Fringe lily, water fringe	*Nymphoides peltata*
Frog fruit	*Phyla lanceolata*

Common Name(s)	Latin Name
Galingale	*Cyperus longus*
Giant rhubarb, Brazilian rhubarb	*Gunnera manicata*
Golden club	*Orontium aquaticum*
Golden spear, variegated rush	*Baumea rubiginosa* 'Variegata'
Greater spearwort	*Ranunculus lingua*
Hard rush	*Juncus inflexus*
Hornwort	*Ceratophyllum demersum*
Horsetail	*Equisetum* spp.
Ivy-leaved crowfoot	*Ranunculus hederaceus*
Japanese sweet flag	*Acorus gramineus*
Lesser spearwort	*Ranunculus flammula*
Lesser water plantain	*Baldellia ranunculoides*
Lizard's tail	*Saururus cernuus*
Marestail	*Hippuris vulgaris*
Marsh marigold, kingcup	*Caltha palustris*
Marsh woundwort	*Stachys palustris*
Meadowsweet	*Filipendula ulmaria*
Milfoils	*Myriophyllum* spp.
Needle spike-rush	*Eleocharis acicularis*
Norfolk reed	*Phragmites australis*
Pennyroyal	*Mentha pulegium*
Pickerel weed	*Pontederia cordata*
Purple loosestrife	*Lythrum salicaria*

Common Name(s)	Latin Name
Ragged robin	*Lychnis flos-cuculi*
Reed canary grass	*Phalaris arundinacea*
Reed mace, bulrush	*Typha* spp.
Sedges	*Carex* spp.
Soft rush	*Juncus effusus*
Spike-rush	*Eleocharis palustris*
Starwort	*Callitriche* spp.
Sweet flag	*Acorus calamus*
Umbrella grass	*Cyperus alternifolius*
Water avens	*Geum rivale*
Watercress	*Nasturtium aquaticum*
Water crowfoot	*Ranunculus aquatilis*
Water hawthorn	*Aponogeton distachyos*
Water hyssop	*Gratiola officinalis*
Water lilies	*Nymphaea* spp.
Water mint	*Mentha aquatica*
Water plantain	*Alisma* spp.
Water spearmint	*Mentha cervina* (Preslia)
Water violet	*Hottonia palustris*
Water willow	*Justicia americana*
Willow moss	*Fontinalis antipyretica*
Yellow flag	*Iris pseudacorus*
Yellow loosestrife	*Lysimachia vulgaris*
Yerba mansa, Apache beads	*Anemopsis californica*

APPENDIX III: MARGINAL PLANT CHARACTERISTICS

Marginal plants / main characteristics	Plant height (cm)	Principal flower colour	Ideal planting depth (cm)	Max depth attained (cm)	Flowering month	
					from:	to:
Acorus calamus	70	Brown	0–5	15	4	6
Acorus calamus 'Variegatus'	70	Brown	0–5	15	4	6
Acorus gramineus	50	Brown	0–5	15	n/a	n/a
Acorus gramineus 'Variegatus'	30	Brown	0–5	10	n/a	n/a
Acorus gramineus 'Ogon'	40	Brown	0–5	10	n/a	n/a
Alisma parviflorum	50	White	5–10	15	5	7
Alisma plantago	60	White	10–20	25	6	8
Anagallis tenella	5	Pink	0	0	6	8
Anemopsis californica	30	White	0–5	10	7	9
Apium nodiflorum	60	White	0–15	30	5	7
Arundo donax 'Aurea'	150	Brown	0–15	20	7	8
Arundo donax 'Variegata'	240	Brown	0–20	30	7	8
Baldellia ranunculoides	10	White	0–2	10	6	8
Baumea rubiginosa	120	Brown	0–15	25	n/a	n/a
Butomus alba	100	White	10–20	30	6	7
Butomus 'Rosenrot'	100	Pink	10–20	30	6	7
Butomus umbellatus	100	Pink	10–20	30	6	7
Calla palustris	15	White	0–10	15	5	6
Caltha leptosepala	20	White	0–2	10	5	6
Caltha palustris	30	Yellow	0–10	15	3	5
Caltha palustris var. alba	20	White	0–2	5	2	4
Caltha palustris var. palustris	60	Yellow	0–10	20	3	5

Marginal plants / main characteristics	Plant height (cm)	Principal flower colour	Ideal planting depth (cm)	Max depth attained (cm)	Flowering month	
					from:	to:
Caltha palustris 'Flore Pleno'	20	Yellow	0–2	5	5	6
Caltha palustris 'Honeydew'	60	Yellow	0–10	15	3	5
Cardamine pratensis	20	White	0–2	5	4	6
Cardamine raphanifolia	30	Pink	0–10	20	4	6
Carex acuta	60	Brown	0–10	20	5	6
Carex acutiformis	70	Brown	0–15	25	5	6
Carex grayi	40	Brown	0	5	5	6
Carex muskingumensis	40	Brown	0–10	15	5	6
Carex panicea	20	Black	0–5	10	5	6
Carex pendula	60	Brown	0	5	5	7
Carex pseudocyperus	50	Brown	0–5	10	5	7
Carex riparia	60	Brown	0–20	30	5	7
Carex riparia 'Bowles' Golden'	50	Brown	0	5	5	6
Carex riparia 'Variegata'	40	Brown	0–15	15	5	6
Cotula coronopifolia	10	Yellow	0–5	15	5	8
Cyperus eragrostis	50	Brown	0–5	10	6	9
Cyperus longus	100	Brown	0–20	30	6	9
Cyperus rotundus	50	Brown	0–5	10	6	9
Eleocharis palustris	30	Brown	0–10	15	5	7
Equisetum hyemale	150	n/a	0–5	15	n/a	n/a
Eriophorum angustifolium	60	White	0–10	15	5	6
Eriophorum latifolium	60	White	0–10	15	5	6
Eriophorum russeolum	20	Brown	0–2	5	5	6
Eriophorum vaginatum	60	White	0–5	5	5	6
Geum rivale	40	Maroon	0	5	4	8
Glyceria cvs	90	Brown	0–20	30	7	8
Gratiola officinalis	30	White	0–10	15	6	8
Houttuynia cordata	20	White	0–5	10	7	9

Marginal plants / main characteristics	Plant height (cm)	Principal flower colour	Ideal planting depth (cm)	Max depth attained (cm)	Flowering month	
					from:	to:
Houttuynia cordata 'Variegata'	15	White	0–5	10	7	9
Iris laevigata cvs	50	Various	0–10	15	5	6
Iris louisiana cvs	80	Various	0–15	25	6	7
Iris pseudacorus	150	Yellow	0–15	30	5	6
Iris pseudacorus other cvs	120	Various	0–10	20	5	6
Iris versicolor cvs	90	Various	0–10	20	5	6
Iris virginica cvs	80	Various	0–5	20	6	7
Isolepsis cernua	20	White	0–5	30	5	8
Juncus effusus	60	Brown	0–5	10	5	7
Juncus effusus 'Spiralis'	30	Brown	0–5	10	5	7
Juncus ensifolius	25	Brown	0–5	15	5	8
Juncus inflexus	80	Brown	0–5	15	5	7
Lathyrus palustris	80	Pink	0–2	10	5	7
Lobelia chinensis	10	White	0–10	15	6	9
Lobelia fulgens 'Queen Victoria'	120	Red	0	5	7	9
Lobelia siphilitica	90	Blue	0	5	7	9
Lychnis flos-cuculi cvs	60	Various	0	2	5	9
Lycopus europaeus	80	White	0–5	15	5	7
Lysichiton camtschatcensis	100	White	0–10	20	4	6
Lysimachia nummularia	5	Yellow	0–5	10	4	9
Lysimachia punctata	60	Yellow	0	5	5	8
Lysimachia thyrsiflora	50	Yellow	0	10	6	8
Lythrum salicaria	180	Purple	0–5	15	6	9
Lythrum salicaria 'Robert'	120	Pink	0–5	15	6	9
Mentha aquatica	20	Purple	0–10	20	6	8
Mentha cervina	20	Purple	0–5	10	6	8
Mentha pulegium	20	Purple	0–5	10	6	8
Menyanthes trifoliata	20	White	5–10	30	4	6

Marginal plants / main characteristics	Plant height (cm)	Principal flower colour	Ideal planting depth (cm)	Max depth attained (cm)	Flowering month	
					from:	to:
Mimulus luteus	90	Yellow	0–10	15	5	7
Mimulus ringens	60	Blue	0–5	10	6	8
Monochoria hastata	150	Blue	0–15	30	7	10
Myosotis palustris cvs	10	Various	0–10	20	4	9
Nasturtium aquaticum	25	White	0–10	20	4	6
Oenanthe cvs	30	White	0–5	20	5	7
Orontium aquaticum	20	Yellow	5–15	40	6	8
Peltandra undulata	30	White	0–10	20	6	8
Penthorum sedoides	30	Green	0–5	15	7	9
Persicaria amphibia	10	Pink	0–20	40	7	9
Phalaris arundinacea	90	Brown	0–15	25	7	8
Phragmites australis	240	Brown	0–15	60	7	9
Pontederia cordata	40	Blue	5–10	20	7	10
Pontederia cordata alba	35	White	5–10	20	7	10
Pontederia cordata lanceolata	150	Blue	5–15	30	7	10
Pontederia cordata 'Pink Pons'	35	Pink	5–10	20	7	9
Potentilla palustris	15	Maroon	0–5	15	6	9
Ranunculus flammula	15	Yellow	0–10	20	6	8
Ranunculus lingua 'Grandiflorus'	40	Yellow	0–10	30	6	8
Rhynchospora colorata	30	White	0–2	10	7	9
Rumex hydrolapathum	120	Brown	0–5	15	6	8
Rumex sanguineus	30	Brown	0–2	10	6	8
Sagittaria graminea cvs	25	White	5–15	25	6	7
Sagittaria latifolia cvs	60	White	5–20	30	6	7
Sagittaria sagittifolia cvs	30	White	5–15	30	6	7
Saururus cernuus	40	White	5–15	25	6	8
Saururus chinensis	30	White	5–10	20	6	8
Schoenoplectus albescens	200	Brown	5–10	30	7	8

Marginal plants / main characteristics	Plant height (cm)	Principal flower colour	Ideal planting depth (cm)	Max depth attained (cm)	Flowering month	
					from:	to:
Schoenoplectus lacustris	240	Brown	5–10	60	7	8
Schoenoplectus zebrinus	100	Brown	0–10	20	7	8
Scrophularia auriculata	120	Maroon	0–5	15	7	8
Sparganium spp.	100	White	0–10	30	6	7
Stachys palustris	90	Purple	0–5	20	7	9
Thalia dealbata	200	Purple	5–15	20	8	9
Typha angustifolia	200	Brown	5–15	30	8	9
Typha gracilis	150	Brown	5–15	20	8	9
Typha latifolia	240	Brown	5–15	50	8	9
Typha laxmannii	150	Brown	5–15	20	8	9
Typha minima	30	Brown	0–5	10	6	8
Veronica beccabunga	10	Blue	0–5	15	5	7
Zantedeschia aethiopica	80	White	0–2	15	6	8

SUGGESTED FURTHER READING

Bardsley, L. (2012) *The Wildlife Pond Handbook*. London, UK: Bloomsbury Publishing.

Chatto, B. (2005) *The Damp Garden*. London, UK: Cassell.

Holmes, C. (2015) *Water Lilies*. Woodbridge, UK: ACC Art Books.

Kircher, W. and Thon, A. (2016) *How to build a Natural Swimming Pool*. London, UK: Filbert Press.

Paul, A. and Rees, Y. (1994) *The Water Garden*. London, UK: Frances Lincoln.

Slocum, Perry D. (1996) *Water Lilies and Lotuses*. Oregon, USA: Timber Press.

Speichert, G. and S. (2004) *Encyclopedia of Water Garden Plants*. Oregon, USA: Timber Press.

USEFUL CONTACTS

SUPPLIERS

Geosynthetic clay pond liners

EcoMerchant
www.ecomerchant.co.uk
01793 847444

Geosynthetics
www.geosyn.co.uk
01455 617139

Hydroclay
www.hydroclay.co.uk
0330 311 2575

Butyl and EPDM pond liners

Gordon Low
www.gordonlowproducts.co.uk
01480 405433

Pond Superstores
www.pondsuperstores.com
01580 241017

Water Gardening Direct
www.watergardeningdirect.com
01778 341199

Pond plant suppliers

Devon Pond Plants
www.devonpondplants.co.uk
01548 521286
ruth@devonpondplants.co.uk

Plant fairs

Plant Hunters' Fairs
www.planthuntersfairs.co.uk
0771 699 0695

Rare Plant Fair
www.rareplantfair.co.uk
info@rareplantfair.co.uk

NATURE AND WILDLIFE ORGANISATIONS

Freshwater Habitats Trust
www.freshwaterhabitats.org.uk

National Trust
www.nationaltrust.org.uk
Properties and gardens owned by the National Trust.

National Garden Scheme
www.ngs.org.uk
Gardens open for charity.

Plants For A Future
www.pfaf.org
A resource and information centre for edible plants.

Royal Horticultural Society
www.rhs.org.uk
Flower shows and events.

Royal Society for the Protection of Birds
www.rspb.org
Advice on attracting birds into your garden.

Plant Heritage (formerly the National Council for the Conservation of Plants and Gardens)
www.plantheritage.org.uk
Garden plant conservation charity.

Natural History Museum
www.nhm.ac.uk/discover/pond-life-facts-about-habitats-plants-animals.html

Environment Agency
www.gov.uk/government/organisations/
environment-agency

GARDEN DESIGN, ENVIRONMENTAL ENGINEERING AND POND SERVICES

DU Waterscapes
www.duwaterscapes.co.uk

Helen Johnson
07879 423894

LandMarc Construction
www.landmarc.co.uk
01803 712946

WildPonds
www.wildponds.co.uk
01328 829309

ACKNOWLEDGEMENTS

I would firstly like to thank my long-suffering wife, Sharne, for the long-standing excuse to get out of household chores: 'I must get on with my book.' Likewise, I owe a debt of gratitude to Ruth, with whom I work, for transformation of my scruffy sketches into the neat and detailed diagrams throughout the book; also her daughter Hester for colouration of the drawings and the illustration of pond bugs in Chapter 10. Many of my customers and contacts have provided photographs via my website which I have used – thank you all. The relevant images are listed here in the order in which they first appear, with apologies to anybody I have omitted. All the other images are my own.

Ruth Aspland: Pp. 10, 17, 19, 23, 26, 27, 28, 29, 31, 53, 62
Kevin Tribe: P. 12
Helen Johnson Garden Design: Pp. 13, 31, 49, 192
Brian Howard: Pp. 14, 34

Ian Wilson, Wild Ponds: Pp. 14, 36
Dee Stewart: P. 15
Catherine Jones: P.16
Brian Oakwell: Pp. 22, 48
Ray Maddock: P. 25
Stephan Harding: P. 25
Toyah Saunders: P. 25
Andrew Bowden: P. 26
Du Waterscapes: P. 40
Joanne Mcintosh: P. 36
Fiona Parrott: P. 36
Alicja Novak: P. 37
Sharon Levett: P. 38
Alfie Vernon: Pp. 45, 46
Niki Sharp Garden Design: Pp. 46, 47
Jim Adamson: P. 51
Jane Calder: p. 74
Amanda Whittaker: P. 186
Hester Aspland: Pp. 190, 194

INDEX